# BRITAIN
## AT
# WAR

4938
This edition published 1996 by Colour Library Direct
© 1989 CLB International, Godalming, Surrey
Printed and bound in Italy by New Interlitho
ISBN 1-85833-577-9

# BRITAIN
## · AT ·
# WAR

### BENNY GREEN

*London children during the 1939 evacuation.*

My war began with a small boy surrounded by strangers in a sunny Hertfordshire garden, and ended with a hulking young man surrounded by loyal friends on the second floor of Lyons' Corner House in Coventry Street, perched on a windowsill looking down on scenes of euphoric bacchanal. Both those moments are etched on the memory, as though for a split second the world stopped turning in deference to the cosmic photographer compiling evidence of a pregnant event. The six years between those two snapshots changed the face of civilisation, recast the map of Europe, wrote some of the most lurid chapters in the long history of the British, saw priceless things go up in smoke and some others reborn.

When war finally arrived, just in time to spoil the end of the English cricket season, it was received with mixed emotions by the British: fear, bewilderment, resolution, truculence, but not much surprise. Whatever the official historians and biographers have had to say about it, the mass of people knew with stoic certitude that a war was coming. They sensed it with growing perception down the long haul of the 1930s. They hoped it would not come, yet they knew it would. When, belatedly it did come, just in time to justify the prognosticators who had been forecasting world war in the Thirties, it was greeted with all the emotions I have described, but also with a curious kind of relief, much as to say that now all the shillyshallying was done with, the country could get down to it and learn the worst. Whether or not Whitehall and Downing Street were similarly aware may or may not be so. There is never any accounting for political self-delusion, and the passage in British political history culminating in the Second World War will be seen by posterity as one of the more ignoble and asinine in our history.

For me the war was profoundly educational even before it started, because it taught me with brutal indifference that all our lives were at the disposal of the State. On September lst, 1939, two days before the end of the uneasy peace, it curtailed my childhood, abruptly, impersonally, slamming the door shut forever on the most impressionable phase of my life, just as, seven years later, it was to announce, with the same callous lack of ceremony, the end of adolescence by bundling me into uniform. As it happened, by so peremptorily expelling me from the courts of childhood, the government was pre-empting the inevitable by no more than eight days. It has escaped the attention of social historians of Britain In the twentieth century that the second war broke out during a temporary break in the nation's educational proceedings. By taking its bow in the school summer holidays, the war flung lives like my own into hopeless

chaos. For the previous eight years I had been attending an elementary school in Upper Marylebone Street, deep in the heartlands of the quadrilateral described by Oxford Street, Tottenham Court Road, Euston Road as it modulates into Marylebone Road, and Baker Street. During my attendance there, the borough councillors of St Marylebone, suddenly mindful of the existence in their midst of a sizeable colony of the poor, decided at last to do something constructive to ease the burden of survival by changing some street names. In 1937, at just about the time that the accession of George VI brought about a boom in the sale of penny Union Jacks, Upper Marylebone Street passed into history, its place usurped by the new-fangled New Cavendish Street, which meant that our school too would have to be rechristened. We soon found ourselves part of Clipstone Junior Mixed, a title which seemed to us as fatuous as it was demeaning, because Clipstone Street marked no more than the location of the school caretaker's house and the back entrance of the premises.

My days at the elementary school had been blissful, but were due to be terminated at last on the ninth day of September by my promotion, if that is the word, to a conspiracy of the higher learning which had better remain nameless, called St Marylebone Grammar School. On a morning in mid July I collected my prize, waved goodbye to the teachers and pupils of the only school I had ever known, and flung myself into a warm bath of football and cricket played on the fields of Regent's Park. For a few weeks I was gloriously unattached to any seat of learning, an old boy of the elementary school, not yet registered as a new one at the grammar school. At which point the war started. Where, educationally speaking, did I belong? There must have been some sort of tacit agreement that any pupil who had yet to enrol at his new school should, in the event of a national emergency, be counted as a member of the old one. Towards the end of August we were all summoned back to school, issued with a list of essential clothing and articles to be packed in a single suitcase, and told to report in the playground the following morning, prepared to be whisked away. The next day the world crisis had not deepened sufficiently for our removal, so we spent the time playing further games of football and cricket. This curious twilight period, neither elementary nor grammar, school nor holiday, peace nor war, ended on the morning of Friday, September 1st. Our parents had been sent due notice of the news that on that morning all of us were to be shipped out of the capital to a place designated no more exactly than as Somewhere in England, the supposition being that this mysterious Somewhere would protect us from the perils of the German Air Force.

But why Hertfordshire? I do not know why, except perhaps that in those remote days the very name of that county possessed overtones of distant rusticity. And so we all marched, labelled and gas-masked, through the streets from school to Great Portland Street Underground station, watched by thousands of moist-eyed women leaning on windowsills and stern-eyed men lounging in doorways. The children were being evacuated. This must surely mean war? When we recognised the point of our embarkation, we assumed a quick trip round the Inner Circle to Paddington, and from there down to the orchards of the West. Instead, we remained on the train until it reached a sort of genteel Sleepy Hollow called Moor Park, where we were ordered to alight and stand in a huge nearby tent with field attached, where a group of ladies from assorted voluntary services were waiting to tick off names, many of which must have seemed to them unpronounceable, and bribe us into compliance with bars of chocolate. Two by two we were driven off in the waiting Wolseleys and Armstrong-Siddeleys to outposts of the Home Counties more opulent than any of us had ever seen outside the cardboard world of Hollywood. I was paired off with a gentle, passive classmate called Max, and taken to a palatial pile a short walk from the station, where, for the next six weeks, we and our billetors coexisted in an atmosphere of mutual loathing. Mr and Mrs D were a childless couple whose only attempt to fructify a barren alliance was to drink gin and play golf. The size of their house obliged them to take in children, but if they had to do their bit for the war effort, they could at least do it with a bad grace.

Much has been made, and I suspect too much, of the sentimental notion that the war brought the classes together. Certainly the evacuation scheme had the effect of flinging disparate sections of society into each other's astonished arms. When Max and I arrived in Moor Park, we were stupefied by the evidence of wealth around us, which seemed so vast as to have nothing to do with us at all. We came from tenements to a detached house with five bedrooms. The drawing room alone was larger than the flat in which I had been living with my parents all my short life. We had been flung out of the crumbling muddle of back streets behind Euston Road, where the appearance of a private car parked outside a domestic cell was exotic enough an *objet d'art* to draw a crowd of goggling juveniles, to a home with two cars in the garage. The first intimations of wealth unbounded had come with the presence outside the tent of a few men wearing the livery of chauffeurs, but the final sensational confirmation that we were, socially speaking, in over our heads came with the presence in the house of one Kathleen, a bespectacled housemaid crisply starched in the green-and-white uniform of her rank, complete with obligatory crown – the lunatic cap designed for the express purpose of letting the underlings know their place. Kathleen soon found our arrival of great convenience in the conducting of her illicit romance with Bill, a perky little peak-capped porter at the underground station. Mr D's garden ran away from

*A policeman carries a very young evacuee. On September 1st, 1939 800 children left Ealing Broadway station for unknown destinations.*

the French windows of the drawing-room across a sleek lawn, past flower beds and a cluster of willows, through a small orchard to the bank of bushes concealing the fence which defined the road on which the station lay. It was a simple trick to pass notes through the fence, and Kathleen quickly recruited the pair of us as willing postmen. She was a frumpy lump, and our eagerness to serve had less to do with any charms she might have had than with our discovery that Mrs D, regarding silken dalliance as something much too good for the servant classes, had forbidden any conduct between the porter and the housemaid.

Two days after our arrival, on a Sunday morning which proved to be part of an Indian summer, Mr D gravely requested our presence in the garden at eleven o'clock. The drawing room wireless was clearly audible through the open French windows, and when Mr Chamberlain began to speak we knew that in some mysterious, unspecified way, a time of danger was about to begin, but not for us, because we had been secreted away in this suburban bolthole. We listened to the

Prime Minister saying that a state of war now existed between Britain and Germany, and then, I think but could not swear, they played the National Anthem. After the broadcast was over, Mr. D began to instruct us in the duties of a patriot, saying that we must conduct ourselves like gentlemen at all times and that a sure sign of the species were shoes whose undersoles had been polished. He then gravely presented us with an elixir of jingoism – a jigsaw puzzle showing the brave resistance of the Welsh Borderers at Rorke's Drift. A little later we heard for the first time the banshee wail of the air-raid siren, and were led to a cupboard under the stairs, where there were stocked so many cases of tinned food, candles, gin and spare golf balls that there was hardly room for us. Then the all clear went and life reverted to the torpor of an English middle-class Sunday.

By the end of that first weekend our new guardians had already decided that the whole business constituted an unfortunate intrusion on their lives. The trouble was that neither Max nor I approximated to the vision which Mr and Mrs D had been carrying around with them ever since being recruited as billetors. The discrepancy became especially painful to Mr D that evening, when his attempt to take us to the local church to pray for victory was undone by the dismaying discovery that he had drawn a brace of infidels in the evacuation sweepstake. He had conjured a scenario of a benign patriarch escorting a pair of chirpy cockneys to the presence of a God whose mighty power would induce a succession of 'cor-stone-the-crows' and 'cor-strike-a-light-guvnor'. This tableau having been mocked by the facts almost before we had crossed the threshold of the house, he retired ruffled, and had no more to do with us during my stay under his roof. On that first evening we wrote letters home revealing the deadly secret of our whereabouts, and went to sleep in the boxroom at the back of the house, where Max promptly upstaged me by bursting into tears. I made a feeble attempt to comfort him, but before I could work up any conviction, we were distracted by the sound of arriving guests. For the next few hours we were royally entertained by the faery tinkling of ice in cut-class, the chatter of strident voices, the slow ooze of dance music and an occasional whoop of laughter. We even ventured out on to the back landing in an attempt to catch what was being said, but for all the sense we could make of it, the visitors might have been talking Serbo-Croat. A few days later Kathleen served the breakfast eggs with tear-dimmed eyes. Bill had gone away to fight the foe. Gradually his image blurred into the figure of Lieutenant Chard leading the resistance to the Zulu hordes on the dining-room table.

After a week or so, we were told to report to a school which lay four miles away, through a long woodland path, and down a road into Croxley. Mr D said the walk would do us good, and so it did, although not quite in the way he meant. The route through the woods was guarded by twin ranks of horse chestnut trees, which meant that our path was strewn with a carpet of conkers, many of them lying there still half-bedded in their husks. Max and I could scarcely credit what we saw. In the world from which we had just been uprooted, conkers meant the acquirement of a poker or chair-leg, to be flung into the foliage of the trees in the Broad Walk of Regent's Park – a deplorable tactic which usually brought the park keepers down upon us. A haul of twelve to fifteen conkers was considered a reasonable harvest. Here, lying at our feet like a burnished carpet, were thousands of the things. Our fortunes were about to be made. The following morning we left for school armed with two empty potato sacks, and before we had gone a hundred yards along the lane both the sacks were full. Even at a knockdown price of twelve conkers a penny, the contents of the sack represented wealth unparalleled. A mirage formed of a future so handsomely subsidised by the conkers that each evening the pair of us could afford to take the train back to Baker Street and enjoy a few hours of the civilised life, it never once occurring to either of us that we had committed the cardinal error of assessing the rustic market according to metropolitan exchange rates. In this new world, conkers were too accessible to have the slightest value, monetary or otherwise. Happily oblivious, we flung the sacks over our shoulders and trudged on towards glory. After fifty yards we stopped trudging and took a short rest. Then we resumed trudging, this time lasting no more than thirty yards before taking another rest. It was Max who suggested that instead of humping the weight of the merchandise in this way, we ought to drag the sacks behind us as we walked. This brilliant ploy was instantly adopted, and it was not till we had covered a further hundred yards that the friction of the bumpy surface of the lane had worn away the bottom of the sacks and lightened our load to the point where no load was left at all. We flung the sacks into the undergrowth, and resumed our way, this being the first and last time in my life that the loot of the entrepreneur attracted me. The incident may also serve as a pretty example of the culture shock imposed upon the townees of the evacuation scheme, thrown into the depths of the countryside.

Six weeks later, my father came down to collect me, with the news that I was at last to join my grammar school. In was a dramatic moment. If Clipstone Junior Mixed had been moved a laughably short distance from the firing line, SMGS had gone too far in the other direction, and, in an excess of self-preservation, had retired from the world to a little Cornish country town called Redruth. The rail journey started from Paddington in the morning, and long before it ended we were chugging through a Stygian landscape obliterated by the blackout regulations. Ours was a smoking carriage, and each of the passengers, when lighting a cigarette, would bend carefully over the match in an attempt to maintain our cover. The exercise was almost certainly pointless. Three weeks before the outbreak of war, the nation plunged itself into darkness in an attempt to assess the effectiveness of the blackout scheme. Next day the Aeronautical Correspondent of *The Times* reported on what he had seen from the vantage-point of a Wellington bomber:

*Newbury had made a fair pretence of darkening itself. It was not enough to wipe it off the map, and the railway station with a line of signal lights beyond it gave us our guide on to the target of the racecourse. Then we turned for the rest of our trials. Motor-car lights showed us the road to Reading. From Reading we could see the glow of London.*

An endearing touch of blimpish absurdity was added by a letter from an irate gentleman in Bishopsgate, who, after composing a brief elegy on the beauty of London unlit, went on:

*In a Berkshire village, in 1939, young London evacuees out for a stroll with their teacher.*

*If the black-out was not, technically, a complete success, it was surely not the fault of the workers, nor can it have been due to any deliberate obstruction by the public. But absentmindedness there must have been. How can one account otherwise for the mellow light, from the basement of the War Office itself, that streamed vertically upwards into the potentially hostile sky?*

By the time of my arrival in Cornwall the blackout regulations were being observed with a religiosity surely passionate enough to have satisfied even the correspondent to *The Times*. But we were so far from the war, and so far beyond the range of most enemy aircraft that the point was academic. One day at dusk a crippled German bomber dropped a stray incendiary on a pile of rubble at the back of the local railway station, and on an ominous Sunday in the week of Dunkirk we went to Falmouth and saw the troopships unloading their cargoes of fugitive Canadian infantry. Once or twice the warning sirens sounded, but I cannot recall for what reason. The widowed lady and her two children on whom I was foisted was so wild a contrast to Mr and Mrs D that it seemed I was living in a different war altogether, on a different planet. Mrs Smith, which I think, by the way, was mere euphemism for obscure domestic irregularities, could ill afford to house cuckoos in the nest, but she had taken in a third-former called Drew, and now myself, because she saw in the few shillings per head which the government doled out for evacuees, a chance to show a small profit. Mrs Smith ran the kind of establishment where you had to ask formal permission before taking a slice of bread and margarine from the plate in the centre of the table. It was the first time I had experienced a poverty more grinding than my own, and I was not altogether grief-stricken when my stay proved to be a brief one. Mrs Smith's only source of income was a boarder, a ninety-year-old survivor from the days when the rivers of the district ran red with the deposits from the local tin mines, and the rum-runners rode the Atlantic breakers to dump their cargoes of dipsomania in the rocky coves of the nearby coast. This ancient deity, Mr Sturt, spent most of the day and night sleeping, although in one of his rare bouts of full consciousness he agreed to give Drew and myself an audience. I remember white hair, bright red cheeks, a thick tweed suit, and skin on the back of his hands silvered by time. He lived on a diet of junket and weak tea, while his only intellectual sustenance was the *Western Morning News*, which he would peer at through the style of eyeglass which Mr Sherlock Holmes was thought by Sidney Paget to have favoured. But the most vital element of the old boy's existence, more life-enhancing than the tea or the junket, more restful than the newspaper, was his sleep, and after a while Mrs Smith was forced to the conclusion that I was too noisy to live under the same roof as he. So I was returned to the evacuee pool and promptly rebilleted two roads and a million miles away, in the detached house of a Mr Griffin, a local panjandrum whose waddling, potbellied eminence was vested in his managership of the local branch of Lloyd's Bank. In some ways he and his wife reminded me of Mrs and Mrs D. They too were childless; they too were golfers. But there, fortunately for me, all resemblance ended. The master of the house exuded a comically Dickensian benignity and soon came to look upon me very nearly as his own child. His wife Muriel, much younger than he, was more like a soft touch of an aunt, and cooked some beautiful meals. She was an unquenchable patriot and, by the time I arrived in her house, was among the most conscientious members of the local ARP, disappearing two afternoons a week on mysterious practice sessions in which buckets of sand were flung on small fires and stirrup pumps distributed to local farmhouses. Their house was in Clinton Road, at that time the smartest thoroughfare in town, and was kept clean by a little maid called Margaret, who bicycled in to work from the hinterlands each morning, wore no trace of make-up, and spoke in a burr which took me several weeks to penetrate to the point where we could sit and chat with each other.

Of course I was wretched and miserable in Clinton Road. It was not at all like Euston Road, and I knew nobody in the school. But the Griffins did everything they could and more to make me comfortable, and it must have been through their numberless small kindnesses that I managed to stick it out with them for about a year. The period with them coincided with the worst catastrophes of the war. It was in the dining-room of the house in Clinton Road that I read of the fall of France, of the raging Battle of Britain, of the bewildering twists of fortune in the Western Desert, of the sudden transformation of the Russians from dirty rats to good guys. When Chamberlain was replaced by Churchill, I gathered from the general mood of the household that this was thought to be a good thing in the muted purlieus of Clinton Road, although Mr Griffin retained a few doubts connected with Churchill's old reputation as a warmonger. As this seemed the ideal qualification for someone leading the nation into a fight for its life, I was amused by old Griffin's caution, and thankful for the extent of his patience with a boisterous young stranger. Only once do I recall his tolerance crumbling. I had just discovered the delicious joke of *Three Men in a Boat*, and was reading the episode of the tin of pineapple in the lounge one teatime when Griffin, intent on the financial pages of *The Daily Telegraph*, flung down the paper and said that if I could not control my laughter I would have to continue reading in the kitchen.

My only real anxiety during this time was that the flow of letters from home, written in my father's dashing hand, would keep on coming in defiance of the lurid news of the nightly bombing of London. The content of the letters was cheerful, and usually concerned with the eccentric doings of his brothers and sisters, sporting affairs, and the ups and downs of life at the greyhound tracks within whose bounds he spent whatever leisure he could purloin from his war work. My father, who had had more than enough foreign travel at the government's expense as a teenager in the Ypres Salient, was now recruited in the national interest at a factory somewhere in the City engaged in the manufacture of military greatcoats. The problem of devising escape routes to the free air of Stamford Bridge and the White City was soon resolved when he converted the two brothers who owned the factory to the study of the science of greyhound racing, after which it seems that the three of them would leave the staff busily engaged on its duties, and repair to whichever track was conducting an experiment.

In the spring of 1941 I returned home to London for the holidays and resolved never to go back, the dangers of bombing seeming to me by now far more acceptable than a dull existence among the hedgerows, so far from familiar things. It may strike the modern reader as absurd that a fugitive from air raids should return to the centre of the target for something as contradictory as a holiday. But this had become common practice among the evacuee population, which had quickly realised that the odds against their destruction were rather longer than those quoted by the politicians of the late 1930s. Certainly the return home was an eye-opener. The boys' club I had attended two evenings a week had been blown to pieces and replaced by a huge tank of water for use against incendiary bombs, and one of the little Nash cottages just inside the northern gates of Regent's Park, where once dwelt the uniformed ogre who guarded his conkers from our chair-legs, had vanished into the past, the only evidence that it had ever existed being a broad patch of charred grass. Most outrageous of all, some lout had dropped a bomb on Clipstone Junior Mixed, slicing away its top story and making a mess of the infants' playground. But this sort of thing apart, the district seemed to be bearing up under the strain well enough. There were even bonuses. On Marylebone Green a barrage balloon was moored to a huge, three-sided mesh arrangement which served admirably in the five-a-side football matches we played there every morning. The best news, however, was that enough contemporaries were available to stage a football match at all. It was this realisation, that life went on in London, that stiffened my resolve never to go back to the home of a stranger.

Even on that first day of departure there had been gaps in the ranks, names which elicited an ominous silence when the roll was called, names sadly crossed off the list by the volunteer Valkyries in the tent at Moor Park, names which simply opted out of national crisis. I was never sure what crime this constituted, and neither were the absconders. Was it a crime at all? Truancy? Not in the middle of school holidays. Desertion? Not from a voluntary scheme. But whatever you called it, there were a few bold spirits who wanted no part of the evacuation and the discomforts to which it might lead. When I arrived home for my holiday it was to find most of my absentee friends conducting their sexual education at a makeshift mixed school just across the road from the Royal Academy of Music. There was in addition a sizeable group of near-contemporaries who by 1941 had left school only a little earlier than the law allowed and were now beyond the reach of the schoolteacher forever more, and it was this nucleus, of absentees and old boys, which supplied the manpower for our sport in the park. About them all there was an elusive cavalier attitude, as though the normal rules of educational procedure, the punishing of truancy, the prosecution for persistent absenteeism, and the dire consequences following the refusal to register with any school at all, were in abeyance, as indeed for all practical purposes they were. I joined a drifting colony of free spirits, and was blissfully happy to realise that in return for bombing and broken nights, it was still possible to enjoy peacetime delights I had assumed to be locked away for the duration. The reference books tell me that the drawn Wembley Cup Final between Preston North End and my beloved Arsenal which my father and I attended took place on May 10th, 1941, and that in deference to the enemy, attendance was limited to 60,000. The same volumes tell me that my first international match, England v. Scotland at Wembley, was played on October I4th of that year before 65,000, and that the return match on the same ground took place on January 17th, 1942. It was on the night of one of those two games that the war, till now, a distant impediment to petty pleasures, suddenly became real.

People tended to make their own arrangements for sheltering from the raiders at night. One of my aunts spent the entire war sleeping on the northbound platform of Regent's Park tube station, where she became a citizen of a bizarre nocturnal township with its own conventions. I have a dim recollection of sheltering with my parents once or twice on the lower floors of a large block of offices facing our block of flats. But on the night when for the first time I savoured the reality of total warfare we were all seated in the cellar of my grandfather's house round the corner. This cellar stretched out under the macadam road surface of Greenwell Street, and may or may not have provided better protection than the cellar under the stair of the house which I always yearned to explore and never did. The final vote went to the cellar

*A bombed street and a shattered lamppost provide a playground for youngsters determined not to let a war interfere with their fun and games.*

under the road because, in the event of a direct hit on the house, we might survive in the cellar under the stairs but be entombed, whereas if a bomb hit the road then we would all go straight up and come down in the open air. That night there was the usual thumping and crumping of the anti-aircraft batteries around the park. The men sat there engrossed in their game of solo, arguing bitterly over each other's tactics, when the whistling descent of high-explosive bombs suddenly became close enough to disturb the spindrift of dust and cobwebs on the ceiling. Then there was a much louder screaming sound, followed by the loudest bang I had ever heard. The foundations of the cellar shifted, and the reverberations of the crash were followed by a frightful clatter of broken glass and flying bricks. I can see and hear my father leaping up and shouting to my grandfather, 'They've hit the house, but we're all right'. Fearful of being buried under the rubble we poked our heads round the cellar door to find the world had gone to hellfire. The night sky was bruised from the reflection of nearby fires, and pencils of criss-crossing light from the searchlights probed the clouds. We could hear people shouting and the wail of sirens, the clangour of fire-engines. But to our amazement, there the house still was. In the long narrow yard running between the entrance to the cellar and the outer walls of the house were a dozen incendiary bombs sputtering on the damp ground. My father grabbed a broomstick and prodded at one in an attempt to perform some obscure function known only to himself. By this time one of my aunts was standing at his side complaining bitterly that in saying the house had been hit he was causing unnecessary anguish to the rest of the family, that he had always been a liar and a troublemaker even as a little boy, and that this whole thing was all his fault. At this point the broomstick burst into flames and my father offered it to her, saying that she, being an old witch, would know what to do with it. He then began emptying buckets of sand over the bombs, and this is how he was discovered by two ARP men who told us all to run for shelter in the building across the way. All this time the guns were banging away to a counterpoint of exploding bombs. We all trooped upstairs into the street, and as we were crossing the road to sanctuary a cluster of incendiaries scattered across our path. It comes back to me that, contrary to my expectations, the fire bombs did not just lie there but fizzed and jumped like so many spitting cats. We picked our way through them and were soon safe underground. It was then that I noticed that my grandfather was still clutching the last hand dealt to him before the interruption to the card game. A week later he was still grumbling that the raid had deprived him of an absolutely certain, cast-iron Abundance. When we emerged into the still smouldering street next morning, it was to see that a huge explosion had blown away half the block, leaving the northern end flattened except for my grandfather's house, which now stood, like the last decaying tooth in a decrepit head, forlorn in the debris of its old

companions. It was a misfortune with consolations, for another of my aunts, the insanely snobbish one, derived much gratification in later years by telling people that her father lived in a detached residence.

By the time of the raid, my father had taken steps to find a suitable school for me, or even an unsuitable one, for nobody knew better than he that a life of constant truancy can bring about the most exotic consequences. His researches had informed him that the stream of boys deserting the evacuation scheme had grown to a flood of such alarming proportions that the authorities had no alternative but to acknowledge the fact by reopening some of the shut-down grammar schools. The historians have tended to shower unqualified praise on the evacuation scheme without ever referring to the truth of the matter, which was that it was at any rate a partial failure in the sense that so many of the participants opted out. As to the resumption of my schooling, I received the news with mixed feelings, seeing that it was inevitable but sorry that it would seriously impede my education, which, in the absence of classroom and curriculum, had begun to flourish at last. By some obscure process, in the months when I was drifting out of the gravitational pull of the schools, I had experienced what some have defined as the birth of intellectual passion, and was beginning to subject myself to a regimen more rigorous by far than any teacher would have thought practical or even feasible. I had become a passionate music student, to my own astonishment as much as anyone else's, and, by the time of the great raid, was already able to render *The Bluebells of Scotland* and *The Sunshine of Your Smile* on the smaller of the two saxophones languishing in my father's wardrobe, dusty symbols of his considerable exploits as a professional musician in the 1920s. To return to school would mean wasting endless hours on Latin and Maths which could more profitably have been spent acquainting myself with the intricacies of improvisation. But at least I was done with the statistics of evacuation once and for all. The experience had been instructive in a way that the normal educational processes could never be. In the space of two years I sampled three social milieus of which in the ordinary way of things I might have remained ignorant, the tipsy upper-middle-class of Mr and Mrs D; the cruel penny-pinching neediness of Mrs Smith; and the professional middle-class decencies of the Griffins. I now settled back into the old life, never suspecting that in becoming a schoolboy once more I was about to be enlisted in a conspiracy of wilful adolescent anarchy so diverting that before long there would be days when I could hardly wait to get to school each morning for fear of missing something especially outrageous. Intimations of the high jinks to come were vouchsafed me even as my father and I walked down the long path back to the trolley-bus depot after our first interview; lagging a pace behind my father, I was startled to see that behind a privet hedge a boy not much older than me was embracing a young lady wearing the blazer of the girls' school next door.

The William Ellis School, named after a heretic whose persistent handling of the ball when playing football had resulted in the codification of a new game called rugby union, sat up on the southern fringes of Parliament Hill Fields, and had been lying barred and shuttered ever since its pupils had been packed off to the country. At some point after the outbreak of war but before we heard about it, William Ellis had been selected as the site for a glorious fiasco called the North London Emergency Secondary School, the repository for all the waifs, delinquents, truants, rebels and petty criminals who had used the incident of evacuation as the pretext for a life of reckless hedonism. Because the teaching staff of William Ellis was either serving in the armed forces or teaching down in the country, the instructors at the NLESS were, to use the kindest of euphemisms, the dregs of the profession, or dotards dragged out of retirement, or young ladies with no suspicion of what they were letting themselves in for. I remained in this madhouse for about two years, by far the most memorable of my school career. Not that I didn't learn anything worth knowing there. I greatly improved my technique as a stopper centre half, was privy to sexual discussions as informative as any I experienced in later life, sharpened my wits in the cause of truancy, was introduced to the unblemished pleasure of running, thanks to the proximity of the Parliament Hill track, and came for the first time to realise that there are clowns in this life whom no restrictive measures can contain, and that when we encounter them we should be thankful.

At the NLESS I encountered at least fifty of the species, among them Woolmer, a goggle-eyed grinning slobberer who spent his lunch breaks wandering about the heath swallowing as many live insects as he could catch, and innocently terrorising old ladies by standing before them and stuffing mouthfuls of grass down his throat. There was Black, T., who, in an attempt to express his idolatry of the then Arsenal centre forward, inscribed his art exercise book with the name of Drake, E., persisting so doggedly with this imposture that when, after a year the art master received the report of Black, T., he complained to the headmaster that no such boy existed, and furthermore, what had happened to the documents concerning Drake, E.? There was Mr Purdy, a one-armed wreck of a teacher whose disabilities, mental as well as physical, caused him to set fire either to himself or the equipment in the chemistry lab two or three times a month. And there was Morecombe, whose truancy was so persistent that some of the teachers claimed never to have seen him, and whose life was so shrouded in mystery that whenever we happened to bump into him and asked him what his game was, he would redden, smirk and light an

evasive De Reszke Minor. All became clear when Morecombe, although no more than a fourth-former, left to get married to the love of his life, a girl at the school next door, who was about to present him with a son and heir. I like to think it was this pair of lovers who had been convening behind the hedge on that first morning I was taken to the school. There was Reece, who openly courted the young Scots lady who arrived one day with the hopeless task of teaching us English Literature. And a very prim-looking bespectacled boy who used plasticine to make a cast of the caretaker's keys and gain access to the school's stationery cupboard. I forget this felon's name, but the innocence of his demeanour, combined with the felonious tendencies of his heart, probably qualified him for a spectacular career in politics.

Since the school's population was drawn from a freakishly wide catchment area, luncheon facilities of a sort were provided, and spurned by most of us. I recall an everlasting mess of potage consisting of diced beetroot, grated carrot and cold potatoes, and can still recall the voluptuous delight of the jam tarts in the log cabin cafe on the heath only a few yards from the back entrance to the school. Most of the boys were living in homes deprived by conscription of fatherly authority, with the result that petty pilfering, insolence, truancy and philandering were facts of life. Even persistent absenteeism could be blamed on the war. Either there was a raid last night, or there was a large hole in the road where your trolley-bus usually passed, or there was yet another family funeral to attend. None of the teachers cared, and the closest thing to academic distinction achieved by my contemporaries was one England amateur football cap, the rise of one of my classmates to the godhead of anchorman on television sports programmes, and my own subsequent drift into the popularity polls of the musical weeklies. We all acquired a sort of tenth-rate sophistication at our local picture palaces, took advantage of clothes rationing to arrive at school each morning as though anticipating an invitation to a fancy-dress ball, and looked forward to the weekly trip out to the school sports ground at Edgware, which entailed a long journey on the Northern Line spent sitting in rapt contemplation of the advertisement for Kent-Cosby hairbrushes, featuring a comely blonde naked from the waist up. This sensational departure from the zippered prudery of the period seems in retrospect to be so incredible that to this day when I mention it, people assure me I must be mistaken. But that blonde amazon gazes down enigmatically still as I type these words, a much welcome addition to the gallery of unforgettable wraiths whose sentimental value is compounded by the sad fact that they comprise all that is left now of adolescence.

The fact that the NLESS was a non-starter culturally speaking might have had a malign effect upon me, although I doubt it. But in the summer of 1942, by now practicing daily on the saxophone, I joined the youth club which had been blown out of its premises by mental defectives in 1940. That establishment had now risen, phoenix-like, from its own ashes to occupy the house next door, and it was within the walls of this warren of a Victorian house that, for the next three years, I furthered my genuine, as distinct from my bogus, education. Here it was that I acquired the ideals of service, of responsibility, of selflessness. Few of the two or three hundred boys who passed through the club in my time succeeded in living up to all the ideals all the time, but most of us tried, and even in failure were at any rate aware that we had failed. It was here that some forgotten, patient elder made me wise in the ways of committees, taught me to take minutes, encouraged me to speak in public. It was here that I mastered the diabolical machinery of pay-telephones, here that I dared to play the saxophone in public for the first time, here that I edited my first and, as it proved, last magazine. These years, blissful as I remember them, coincided with the slow but steady rise in the fortunes of war. When I first enrolled in June 1942, the night raids had fallen off, the Russian army appeared to be making a nuisance of itself, the news from North Africa was more encouraging, and there were now the Americans. By the end of that year London was full of them, thousands of country bumpkins and city slickers trying to fumble their way through the labyrinth of the blackout to whichever watering hole they had been advised by their buddies to seek out. One Stygian night in 1943, one of them unwittingly put our ideals to the test, with ambivalent results. I and a colleague of mine called Ostacchini, currently engaged in certain physical exercises which were supposed to turn him into Denis Compton, were approached by a GI in Euston Road who wished to find an establishment called, I think, Murray's Club. It so happened that I knew exactly where this place was, having attended it a few times in ill-fated attempts to impress other musicians with my playing. So the pair of us offered to guide this personifcation of all Hollywood's glamour through the night to his destination. As we strolled, so we smalltalked, and we were somewhere in the alleys approaching Shaftesbury Avenue when our hero made a casual remark encompassing so many levels of racial bigotry that Ostacchini and I, peering at each other through the murk, expressed mute astonishment. The young soldier then made another observation which made us wonder which side he thought he was fighting on. A further glance between us was enough to seal our man's fate. Leading him into one of the crippled alleys which lose their way down the maze between Oxford Street and Shaftesbury Avenue, we told him he was at journey's end and melted into the blackness. Had we been true to the ideals inculcated into us we would have attempted to reason with him; instead we scuttled off home, agreeing that by spurning his offer of sixpence we had done enough for the moment in the cause of charitable labours.

Because the threat of air raids had receded, precautions at the youth club tended to be woolly, but when in the summer of 1944 the pilotless planes known as doodle-bugs made their appearance in the skies, life once again took on a minatory aspect. One morning in Goodge Street I spent an hour or two helping demolition men clear away the rubble and broken glass which were the legacy of the descent, earlier that morning, of a doodle-bug. There was a girl living in the street whom I was anxious to impress, and had she lived in some other street I fear I might not have been quite so eager to serve. But the one surviving snapshot of that morning is not of the girl at all, but of a large bloodstain on the pavement just outside the entrance to Rawlings, the confectioners and stationers. One of the Rawlings girls had been in my class at Clipstone. How could the hounding of so innocuous a creature possibly be part of anybody's grand design?

There were other obtrusions of the war into the petty pursuits of growing up. One afternoon I stole time from my musical studies to attend Lord's, where an Army side was playing the RAF. During the Army innings the drone of an approaching doodle-bug became too loud to ignore. Then the drone stopped and its descent began, directly, it seemed, over the field of play. Perched up in the Mound Stand, there was neither anywhere sensible for me to run, nor enough time to get there, but the cricketers took what precautions they could by flinging themselves full-length on the turf, heads cradled in hands. Then came the crump from nearby Albert Road, where the bomb had landed. Play then resumed, and, amid mighty cheering, the incumbent batsman, Jack Robertson of Middlesex, hooked the first post-explosive delivery for six. My own cricketing fortunes too were influenced, though more marginally, by the threat of bombing. At the bumpy ground on the northeastern rim of London, on whose unbarbered turf we played inter-club matches on Sunday afternoons drifting into the late dusk of double summertime, the boundaries were defined by dugouts, placed there to provide cover should it be needed. The trenches were never put to their intended use, but proved a match-winning asset at least once. The rules of our league stipulated that if both sides had completed an innings by five o'clock, then the contest became a two-innings match. One Sunday we bowled out a side from Cambridge Heath for about thirty, and then scored twice that total as five o'clock approached. At five minutes to five our number eleven struck a beamer to the boundary and nobody could find the ball.

By the time the search was abandoned, it was long past five and the game over. That evening one of our supporters confessed that he had tapped the ball into one of the trenches, safe from the prying eyes of the opposition. A more sentimental amendment to the normal routine was to be found in Regent's Park, where the removal of most of the railings defining its perimeter turned the place into a round-the-clock trysting ground. By the time of the doodle-bugs, my educational status had altered yet again. The main body of SMGS, having belatedly realised that I was right, had by now gathered up what was left of its sons, decamped from Cornwall and returned to the dusty nest in Marylebone Road, calling in all its vagrant old boys as it did so. These included me, and I now found myself deprived at a stroke of saunters across Parliament Hill, of jam tarts in the little rustic cafe, of pyromaniac chemistry instruction, of the sinuous stripper with the hairbrush, of Woolmer and Black and the rest of the slapstick players in the farce of the NLESS. Instead I found myself transplanted to an environment which did what it could to ape the manners, or at any rate the mannerisms, of a public school. If the riotous mockery up on the hill had tended not to take itself seriously enough, SMGS approached the pageant of its own daily routine with all the solemnity of a diocesan convention. Having by now grown to roughly twice the size I had been in Cornwall, and rendered soigne, comparitively speaking, by my experiences as an apprentice jazz musician and hyperactive club member, I found the change uncongenial and at times unacceptable. On D-Day, at morning assembly, our headmaster, one of nature's windbags and a man always prepared to try plugging himself into the global circuit, delivered a bumbling Ciceronian address about the grave importance of what was happening out there on the beachheads, and that we must all do our bit by wearing the school cap in the street and come to school with our shoes polished. That was the week that two Sinatra recordings, *This is a Lovely Way to Spend an Evening* and *I Couldn't Sleep a Wink Last Night* were riding the popularity charts. Perhaps they still were when our leader railed against the 1944 Education Bill as a measure which would prove to be a calamity for institutions like ours. Within twenty years, thundered our leader, the English grammar school would have the barbarians at the gates. As most of us whom he was addressing were precisely the sort of barbarians he had in mind, the speech seemed to me maladroit even for him. In any case, what did we care what happened to this place in twenty years? We were poised on the brink of General School Certificate and ascent to the sixth form. Soon the quaint farce of our education would be done with forever, and those of us like myself whose intellectual curiosity had not quite been murdered by the attentions of pedagogues could get on with our studies.

*During the 1940 blitz a steel-helmeted postman, unable to deliver mail to houses in a bombed street, makes appropriate notes.*

At the club a very different situation prevailed. At least half the membership was at work, and there were several boys who suddenly found themselves, of all things, coal miners. The Minister of Labour of the moment, a man whose phsyical appearance was hideous even for a politician, and who was altogether too fat ever to find a pit-shaft generous enough to accommodate him, had decreed that if the youth of the nation could be made to dig coal, this would in some obscure way speed the victory. Three of my contemporaries were thus drafted and found themselves in Staffordshire, where, liberated at last from the trammels of parental solicitude, they made rapid progress in the pursuit of worldliness when not performing the menial clerical pithead duties for which their literacy qualified them. All three of them would return home for the weekend whenever there was a key cricket or football match to be played, or an especially inviting dance to attend. As the war raced towards its close, they seemed, those three, to be among us more frequently than they ever had been before, joining the rest of us in savouring the anticipation of peace when the threat of being blown to pieces would seem like part of another life, which to some extent it already was.

And so to the day the war formally ended, and the three miners manque and myself drifted with the tide into Piccadilly Circus and found a vantage point on the second floor of Lyons' Corner House, where we gazed down on the hysteria beneath us with the mixed emotions of young men who have been saved from the fighting but whose adolescence was running away now at an alarming pace. How much had we understood of the historical process of the foregoing six years? Some but not much, although there was a vague, unexpressed suspicion shared by all of us that nothing would ever be quite the same again. We had learned by now that nothing ever is. But this was different. It was not only we who had aged, but the country we lived in also. It might have been too fanciful for any of us to have said at the time, but from the moment in 1903 when the Wright brothers achieved a few yards of powered flight in the wilds of Ohio, the days of the British Empire were numbered. For that empire had been impregnable because of two geo-political accidents, the richness of its mineral deposits and the seas surrounding it. All of us, the Smiths and the Griffins and Max and my three coal-mining friends, the crazy boys at the NLESS and my nervous aunt who made a wartime home in an underground station, the girl I loved for a few enchanted days in Goodge Street, and all the aspiring young musicians whose admiration I had so zealously attempted to elicit, all of us had been living our lives on a lump of coal surrounded by water. So long as Britain possessed what other nations believed to be an invincible navy, it could laugh at its enemies and stoke the engines of the Industrial Revolution with cheap coal. But even as the war was racing to its close, the victors were bearing down on the world's oilfields. In any case, the old idea of the Island Race had been rendered comically passé. There were no islands any more. The most insignificant banana republic, provided it could muster one plane and one pilot to fly it, was capable of striking at the very heart of the most powerful nation in the history of the world. A lone airman could circumvent the once impenetrable barrier of the Royal Navy simply by flying above it. And not only was Britain no longer militarily inviolable, its women and children were to be flung into the front line, as all of us had been since the days of the Battle of Britain.

The unspeakable horror of this predicament had penetrated almost nobody's mind until the war actually started. And of those who did have some inkling of what might happen, many over-reacted to the brink of hysteria. After an air exercise which suggested that seven out of every ten bombers will reach their targets, the Prime Minister, Stanley Baldwin, had said: 'The old frontiers are gone. When you think of the defence of England, you no longer think of the chalk cliffs of Dover, you think of the Rhine'. We did recall reading accounts of air raids on Britain during the Great War, but it all seemed very small beer. In 1914 fuel tanks were too small and bomb-aiming devices too crude for the aerial bomber to be much of a threat. And yet even then there had been a few small voices crying in the wilderness. What if Mr Baldwin and Mr MacDonald and Mr Chamberlain had listened to those voices? Might the Blitz have been a less bloody affair? We will never know, but one day, long after the night we perched on that second-floor windowsill celebrating the narrowness of our escape from the grinder of history, I caught the echo of one of those voices, irrelevant now, and mouthing mere sad platitudes – except that what is a platitude this week may well have been a stroke of blinding perception last Tuesday.

On the night of September IIth, 1915, a literary journalist called Henry Major Tomlinson, sickened by the obscenity of what he has seen in Flanders Fields, his hearing permanently affected by the ceaseless thunder of artillery, crosses from France to Fleet Street, reports to his editor before retiring to wife and family in suburbia, safe at least for the moment from the murderous follies of mankind. It is late at night. The children are asleep, and Tomlinson sits in perfect contentment reading a book about the antiquity of Man (a typical Tomlinson touch, that, letting us know precisely what he is reading). Soon his idyll is disturbed by the crump of big guns. He opens his front door to find searchlights fanning the London sky, probing for a zeppelin. The quarry is found. Bombs drop in the distance. The danger recedes, and Tomlinson retires for the night. But he is too troubled to sleep. Instead he pursues his thoughts:

*War now would be not only between soldiers. In future wars the place of honour would be occupied by the infants, in their cradles. Men will now creep up after dark, ambushed in safety behind the celestial curtains, and drop bombs on the sleepers beneath, for the greater glory of some fine figment or other.*

Even as he is thinking these alarming thoughts, there is a great crash. The zeppelin has returned to drop more bombs. Tomlinson bundles his family into the cellar and goes into the street to investigate once again. A nearby villa is in flames. Ambulances arrive. Gradually normality returns:

*…we found ourselves gazing at the familiar and shadowy peace of our suburb as we have always known it. It had returned to that aspect. But something had gone from it for ever. It was not, and never could be again, as once we had known it. The security of our own place had been based on the goodwill or indifference of our fellow-creatures everywhere. Tonight, over that obscure and unimportant street, we had seen a celestial portent illuminate briefly a little of the future of mankind.*

Forty years after that apocalyptic vision of what we were all in for, a cluster of noisy laughing young men perched high over the exultant crowds and looked forward to a future of unbroken peace. Their euphoria was nobly expressed years later by Professor Alan Taylor, in *English History, 1914-45*:

*In the second World war the British people came of age. This was a people's war. Not only were their needs considered. They themselves wanted to win. Future historians may see the war as a last struggle for the European balance of power or for the maintenance of Empire. This was not how it appeared to those who lived through it. The British people had set out to destroy Hitler and National Socialism - "Victory at all costs". They succeeded. No English soldier who rode with the tanks into liberated Belgium or saw the German murder camps at Dachau or Buchenwald could doubt that the war had been a noble crusade. The British were the only people who went through both world wars from beginning to end. Yet they remained a peaceful and civilised people, tolerant, patient and generous. Traditional values lost much of their force. Other values took their place. Imperial greatness was on the way out; the welfare state was on the way in. The British Empire declined; the condition of the people improved. Few now sang "Land of Hope and Glory". Few even sang "England Arise". England had risen all the same.*

My recollections of the period comprise not a portrait of the war as it appears in history but of the time of war during which it happened that I was revelling in my teens. The official chronicles talk of death and deprivation, of hardship and grief, of the blood, sweat and tears of Churchillian oratory. All of that was true, yet little of it touched me. I was in short trousers when the war in Europe started, still only seventeen when it ended. Rationing of food and clothing was stringent enough, but I cannot recall ever going hungry. The cafe on Parliament Hill always seemed stocked with jam tarts and cheese rolls, and at the youth club's cosy if microscopic canteen they dispensed baked beans on toast for fourpence; a slice of toast and jam with a cup of tea cost twopence. There were cafes and restaurants all over London, thousands of them, provided only that you could pay the bill, and if you couldn't, there was always the local fish-and-chip shop. You could, even in the most beleaguered days, eat five or six meals a day if that was how your fancy took you. The war for me and my friends was a time of acquiring techniques and gaining experiences which were to sustain us for the rest of our lives, a time of stumbling enraptured on the existence of pure romance, of contriving to half-fall in love at regular intervals, of doubling in physical size, of realising that music and literature were not chores but joys, of dashing casually towards a sort of pragmatic connoisseurship of the cinema. Whether or not all this was disloyal of us, or insensitive, or doltish, I leave to others, but for us the time of war happened to coincide with a blissfully happy and fulfilling adolescence. Were it not to seem too indecorous, I might be tempted to subtitle this memoir: *The Best Years of My Life*. And the oddest thing of all is that never once in all those six years did it ever so much as occur to me that we might ultimately lose the war, or that I might not be there to see its ending. And so we perched on the windowsill of flowering adolescence revelling in the happy ending beneath us. A few weeks later an atomic bomb was dropped on Hiroshima.

**Benny Green.**

*A Union Jack, hoisted in a gesture of defiance following an air raid, was split in half during subsequent bombing but continued to flutter valiantly amidst the ruins.*

# 1939

One of the first, and certainly one of the most dramatic signs that the war was indeed a reality, was the spectacular about-face performed by Beaverbrook Newspapers. Throughout the later 1930s Lord Beaverbrook (1879-1964) had vigorously crusaded for a succession of political non-starters, ranging from Imperial Preference and the formation of the abortive United Empire Party, to the espousal of the cause of Edward VIII, and a policy of European isolation for a Britain sufficiently heavily armed to deter any potential enemies. A year before this photograph was taken, on the eve of the Munich Conference, the *Daily Express* carried the front-page assurance: 'There will be no European war'. Four weeks later, after the Conference, which had managed to delay the start of the war in return for the dismemberment of Czechoslovakia, the message was the same: 'Britain will not be involved in a European war this year, or next year either'. Indeed, so passionately isolationist was Beaverbrook that he had not approved of Britain attending the Conference at all: 'Chamberlain put pussy in the well. It is quite true that we owe him gratitude for pulling pussy out again'. On January 18th, 1939, Beaverbrook's papers announced: 'Britain has nothing to fear at home or abroad'. As late as August 11th, 1939, it was 'Britain will not be involved in a European war'. Hence the dramatic nature of the paper seller's placard announcing the *Sunday Express* news that Britain was after all at war.

The news was evidently more of a surprise to his lordship than to the bulk of the British population, which, desirous though it was for a continuance of its rickety peace, has a nasty feeling after 1936 that some time soon there would be another war with Germany. The stoic publicist with copies of the *Sunday Express* dated ominously 'September 3rd, 1939' under his arm is standing in the Strand at the heart of London, a street curiously symbolic of the mood of the town. In the 1920s the Liberal editor A.G. Gardiner defined it as the most attractive street he knew, in which people 'hurried in pursuit of some sunlit adventure of the soul'. Ten years later George Orwell was deeply depressed by the place. He would be. Gazing at the traffic and the pedestrians, he wrote: 'Enough noise to waken the dead, but not to waken this lot'. Now, on the brink of another new decade, the paper seller's message puts to rest once and for all the old music hall bromide:

*Let's all go down the Strand,*
*Oh, what a happy land.*

On this sunlit, tragic morning the pavements are virtually deserted.

Monday, September 4th. Business as usual, except that there has been a significant addition to the accoutrements of a gentleman. Last week it was rolled umbrella and a folded copy of *The Times*. Now it is rolled umbrella, folded copy of *The Times* and gas-mask. The little cardboard box has overnight become a sign that the British mean business. The young man on the left, faintly reminiscent of Bertie Wooster on the morning after a night on the tiles, clutches his box with the aspect of a man considering whether or not to throw it at the photographer. His companion, grim in the face of peril, marches resolutely on, across London Bridge, fighting his last-ditch fight on behalf of the doomed bowler hat. On the following afternoon two young secretaries escape from the office – and from the dictation of men like the pair crossing the bridge – and go to Hyde Park, where the sun, as though aware of adjustments to the nation's prospects, does what it can by providing an Indian summer by way of consolation. Something which dates this photograph is the evident faith of the young ladies in the honesty of their fellow-Londoners. One of them sleeps on, her handbag lying unattended on the grass beside her. Perhaps she is reassured by the proximity of that British bulldog, displaying all the panoply of war.

One commodity of war which can never be in short supply is sand, which stretches for mile after mile around the perimeter of the island. At Hornsea, holidaymakers do their bit by contributing to the figure of 60,000 sandbags urgently required for the barricading of local hospitals. Men in braces, and one woman still smartly straw-bonnetted, help dig up the beach, surrounded by youngsters delighted to discover that mucking about on the seashore has suddenly received the solemn sanction of war work. But not all the trippers are bothering to assist. Some remain staunchly rooted to their deck chairs, some stand and watch the comic spectacle of grown men playing at mud pies. Others queue for the pleasure to be derived from Olicana Cream Ices. But nobody has time to smoke, in spite of the sign attached to the tea-hut, which anxiously advises: 'For your throat's sake smoke Craven A'. The bunting flops weakly in the heat over the hut, and in the right foreground a small girl ponders the extraordinary ways of a world which suddenly decides to bag up all its sand and dump it on the promenade.

Meanwhile, over at Brighton, where the beach is pebbled and useless for sandbags, the younger generation enjoys itself on the first Sunday of the war. Mother rummages in her paper bag for vestigial remnants of lunch, but most of the kids have gone for a dip in the sea, leaving a plentiful supply of gas-masks at the disposal of the junior member, who is, as the saying goes, out of it, but still manages to qualify as the only Briton ever to put his gas-mask to practical use, in this case by propping up his feet on it. The label attached to the box on his left tells us that the party has come down from London. One last day of peace snatched from the jaws of war.

From the moment war was declared, petrol became a vital defensive and offensive weapon. Without petrol, neither tanks nor aeroplanes nor staff cars would be of the slightest practical use. Later in the war, when the great tank battles were waged, the world was astonished to see the most brilliant offensives grind innocuously to a halt, not because of casualties or the accuracy of enemy gunfire, but because there was no fuel left in the tanks. When these pictures were taken in London, at ten minutes to three on Monday afternoon, September 5th, the hastily improvised brew, 'Pool Spirit', was just on the market, at a price likely to draw groans of envy from the motorists of a later age, but which seemed stiff enough at the time. Britain in 1939 was still a society in which possession of a motor car was an indication of an above-average income. In 1928, 40,000 cars had descended on Epsom on Derby Day, but for all that, the streets of British towns were still plentiful with horses. In the 1930s had come speed limits, driving tests, Belisha beacons, and several other refinements aimed at regulating the slowly growing army of drivers, but still the annual number of deaths remained above 6,000. In Parliament and the army there survived many influential figures who believed in the cavalry charge, but they were soon to be discredited as the nature of the new war disclosed itself. Of course, there would always be those who propagated the cause of cars propelled by means other than petrol. During the war there were always a few cars on the road which were dwarfed by the huge bags attached to the roof. It was a sort of alternative, but on the whole it was so much hot air.

From 1927, with the invention of talking pictures, to 1954, when the shadow of television began to darken the prospects of the cinema, films were an essential constituent of daily life in Britain. Every district had several cinemas belonging to rival chains, from which the public could choose. Millions of tickets were sold each week. The faces of Gable and Cagney, of Dietrich and Garbo, were as familiar as the reflection which looked back at you in the mirror each morning. The American studios were like vast repertory theatres which provided the public with its archetypes. The picture palaces supplied more than entertainment, they offered a universal mythology accessible even to illiterates. Any sudden deprivation of the endless belt of mystery, romance, comedy and adventure would be intensely painful to a population which had become dependent on it for its avenues of escape. The British could survive without bananas, tinned salmon and tangerines, but could they carry on without Mickey Mouse and Ginger Rogers? When the Home Office unwisely closed Britain's cinemas, the industry was quick to send a deputation to plead its case, as it happened, successfully. In the meantime, on September 8th, 1939, the menials employed at a Harrow Road cinema show their defiance, not just of Germany, but of the Home Office too.

The Home Office's action was understandable. The fear of mass bombings hung like a bestial threat over the ominously peaceful skies of the capital. By the end of September, most of the great public buildings in London were embattled fortresses braced against the coming onslaught. The deployment of thousands of sandbags at a London hospital, when portrayed through a bird's-eye view, lent a new perspective to the photography of realism.

The musky aroma of dusty sacking and damp sand quickly pervaded the city air. The newspaper seller who has pitched camp outside a bank sits at ease under a carapace of sandbags, dispensing copies of a long-vanished paper called *The Daily Sketch*, whose back page offers the riveting news that the nation now has a Minister of Economic Warfare.

A far sadder irony attaches to the Holborn Restaurant, seen here in the first month of the war with the sandbags packed neatly against its large ground floor windows. The Holborn made an imposing building, yet it is not so much glanced at by the passers-by. The bespectacled, bowler-hatted, bow-tied, cigarette-smoking gent grips his umbrella and marches by, looking resolutely away from the gastronomic temptations to his right. Would he and the rest of the pedestrians have been so indifferent had they been able to read the future? The Holborn Restaurant was a vast emporium incorporating fifteen dining halls ranging from a vast, three-tiered chamber lit with huge chandeliers, to the intimacy of small, private dining chambers. Incongruously, the building also contained no fewer than three Masonic temples. The place was a London landmark which is glimpsed in several biographies of the period. Perhaps its most famous visitor was the young Bernard Shaw. The Holborn Restaurant survived the war but proved no match for the speculative developers of the postwar years. In 1955 it fell before the advancing demolition gangs of the new age.

After Munich, the government, having delivered peace with honour, began delivering peace with air-raid shelters, which were cheap to produce and hardly seemed worth erecting, so frail did they appear. As early as February 1939, much was made of a housewife on the Wilbraham Estate in Manchester, who was publicised as the first woman in the north of England to receive an air-raid shelter. Mrs Ferguson, of 3 Thornleigh Road, looking rather like the matriarch in a Howard Spring novel, smiles uncertainly, as well she might under such remarkable circumstances. Being given something for nothing by the government was not a pleasure to which the general population was accustomed. Even her small dog seems quizzical.

But at least Mrs Ferguson had a back yard in which to erect the shelter. Not all her fellow plebs were as fortunate. The Storeys and the Lawrences, with the war now two months old and nowhere to put their Anderson shelters, decided to build them inside the home, saying that the presence of the structures inside the room caused little inconvenience. 'We regard them as part of the furniture', said the two wives, taking tea for the benefit of the photographers, who may well have supplied the cosmetic jam tarts. It remains unknown whether Sir John Anderson, the politician who gave his name to the mass-produced shelter, was obliged, like the Storeys and the Lawrences, to build his in the kitchen.

Once again the photographic images swing between peace and war to reveal a hinterland which is neither one thing nor the other. The businesslike rangefinder, shrouded in tarpaulin and ringed by protective sandbags, was already in position in the last days of August 1939. But the distinctly festive-looking blonde in the tin hat is an authentic London war worker. So is the guard with the finely-chiselled features on a central London roof, armed with what looks very much like a football supporter's rattle but which is in fact a primitive early-warning device. The roof belongs to the Grosvenor House Hotel, in Park Lane, reputedly one of the safest constructions in London, complete with a ballroom which became a sort of plutocratic air-raid shelter for those who could afford the prices. Pickets, like the man on the roof, were on constant duty, and deep down among the bombproof rooms was a first-aid post with a doctor in attendance.

The young lady obliging the photographer by pretending to powder her cheek is Miss Judy McCrae. It is September 30th, 1939, and Miss McCrae is gainfully employed as a showgirl in a London theatre. But which one? We can only speculate. Perhaps she was rehearsing at the London Palladium with the Crazy Gang in *The Little Dog Laughed*. Or was hoofing it in *Black Velvet* at the Hippodrome. Or was she in *Shepherd's Pie* at the Princes? The issue remains one of the great enigmas of war. All that can be said of the decorative Miss McCrae with any confidence is that she wore a horseshoe for luck, and that she was happy in her work as a warden in Paddington.

Ever since Munich the British generals had been demanding Conscription for National Service, a measure which the government delayed for several reasons, the most alarming of which was that even had they called up a million men, they had nothing with which to equip them. Not till April 1939 did Chamberlain agree to conscription, after which the implementation of the scheme crawled so slowly that by May 1940, when Churchill became Prime Minister, registration of men had reached only to the age of 27. For those impatient to do their bit, there was always the Local Defence Volunteers, who hastily transmuted themselves into the Home Guard. As late as October 1940 this bespectacled patriot, having volunteered for the Home Guard, registers for conscription at a London office.

As for the veterans proudly guarding an armoured car with an ominous numberplate, what would these solemn defenders of the faith have said had they known that the time would come, within their own lifetime, when their dedication to the defence of the realm would flower into one of the nation's favourite jokes? A generation after the war, when many of the Home Guard stalwarts were still alive, the country rocked with laughter at the antics of *Dad's Army*, a group of intrepid television actors simulating the actions of the real volunteers. The Home Guard was not quite a joke, but its usefulness was questionable. As the Oxford History of England puts it, 'it provided a welcome activity for veterans of the First World War'. By the summer of 1940 it had a million members but no rifles. At last, thanks to Lease-Lend, America supplied half a million rifles to the force. This left one last problem. The force still had no ammunition. It is no surprise that this well-intentioned army was eventually distilled into the endearing buffoonery of Captain Mainwaring and his band of old crocks.

The war which was to thrust small children into the firing line began benignly enough. The sandbagging scene, 'Somewhere in London', was commonplace enough. Children were, after all, the most experienced handlers in the country when it came to manipulating bodies of sand, and there were countless occasions like this one when they took advantage of the threat of air raids to assist the military in the tedious duty of bagging sand. In the panic of the moment, no sand was safe, and in this scene the contents of a sandpit in a children's playground is being conscripted for military service. Some idea of the state of Britain's preparedness for total war is conveyed by the fact that the operation appears to be proceeding without benefit of shovels.

A more efficient operation was taking place on September 11th, 1939 at Hyde Park Corner, under the stony gaze of a veteran of an earlier war to end all wars. The statue, one of the finest of all London's war memorials, is in honour of the Royal Artillery. The white mass of Portland stone pointing to the sky is a lifesize 9·2 inch howitzer, flanked at three sides by an artilleryman. On the fourth side, out of sight of the camera, lies a fourth gunner, dead, with the inscription: 'Here was a royal fellowship of death'. The words were to be re-echoed many times before this new war was over, and yet in 1925, when the statue was first unveiled, most people genuinely believed that major wars were now a thing of the past — most people usually do.

One of the many bewildering contradictions of British official policy regarding the likelihood of war is embodied in the fact that although the later 1930s were the years of appeasement at almost any price, as early as 1935 voices were raised in the corridors of power that plans for the rationing of food should be implemented. And yet once the war started, Chamberlain refused to ration food because of the panic it might cause among the population; evidently Chamberlain believed that hunger brought about by an inequality in the distribution of food would not cause panic, or not as much as would a fair-shares-for-all system. Had the Germans launched full sea and air attacks immediately the war started, Britain might have been in serious difficulties. As it was, pressure brought about by the Ministry of Food speeded the process. But although by January 1940 ration books had already been printed, the Food Ministry remained confused as to which system to impose. It eventually opted for the antiquated method of linking consumer to retailer, for no better reason that this method had worked in 1917. In October 1939 the National Registration returns were being used as an aid to the preparation of ration books for distribution. Four young ladies at the Food Executive Office in London work through the lists, and on the first day of rationing a housewife is seen committing herself to the retailer of her choice. The presence of the ubiquitous Mr Heinz and the Express Dairy lend a touch of reassurance to the scene.

One of the more contentious problems facing the War Cabinet was to decide who was for them and who against. Between 1933 and the outbreak of war, thousands of refugees had fled to Britain from countries already being barbarised by the Germans. Were these people potential enemy agents, or had their experiences evolved them into jingo patriots? When war came, all aliens were required to register. Those considered to be a threat to national security, sometimes wrongly, were interned for the duration; the lucky ones were required to report regularly to their local police station. Within hours of the declaration of war, a long queue wound its way down the side of Bow Street police station – all aliens waiting to register. In the leafy purlieus of Golders Green, the immigrant element proved so large that a local church was commandeered as a temporary registration office. But there were some foreign nationals as eager to leave as those in the queues were desperate to stay. On September 4th, the S.S. *Athenia* went down under the assault of U Boats. More than 300 Americans were on board, but despite this mindless tragedy, the day of the sinking saw the United States Shipping Office in the Haymarket besieged by Americans attempting to book passages home. There proved to be so many of them that the office was closed for the day. Meanwhile, the well-off among the British were still taking advantage of unrevised currency laws to transfer not themselves but their money to America.

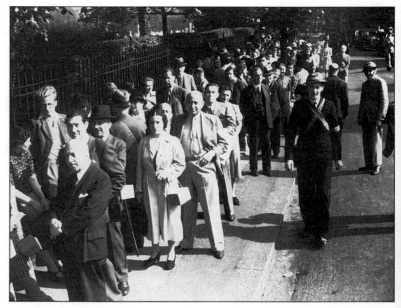

Without question, the one measure which brought home to the population the reality of war was the removal from the major cities of the children. The moment the German Army crossed the Polish frontier on September 1st, evacuation plans were implemented which had been rehearsed for several days before the actuality. As August drifted to a close and with it the era of peace, the schoolchildren of Britain spent the fag end of their summer holidays playing in their school playgrounds, prepared for instant despatch should war come. When it did arrive, the streets of the big cities were already childless. On September 1st, half a million children, recruited school by school, marched from their playgrounds to designated transport centres, from which they were sent on to rural boltholes. The complexity of the scheme and its successful execution was the first planning triumph of the wartime government, but more profound than the removal to 'safe' areas was the effect the evacuation scheme was to have on tens of thousands of its beneficiaries. Many slum children had never seen the sea, never stepped into a field, and the effect upon them of new environments was either so benign that they never returned to the town, or so disastrous that before long they opted out of the scheme and returned home. Their surrogate parents, or 'billetors', as they were defined, received a nominal sum per head to help feed their charges, and in many host areas local schools operated a shift system in a brave attempt to cope with a register of pupils which had been doubled overnight. At Ealing Broadway tube station, a Special Constable sporting a moustache which had suddenly become unfashionable, reassures one of the 800 local children setting out for a destination unknown. But down at King's Cross there are tears and bafflement. Winton Street School is taking to the hills, and it is all too much for one of its less mature students. Freddie Soper, where are you now?

But the evacuation scheme, conceived in such detail and executed with such precision, soon became subject to pressures which none of the administrators could have forseen. The rain of bombs which made the removal of the children such an urgent priority, where was it? As the weeks of the Phoney War slipped eerily by and still none of our major cities and towns was subjected to aerial bombardment, parents and children alike began to wonder. Was it for this peculiar twilight war, this odd life of unpeace, that there had been all this upheaval, emotional as well as geographic? Had families been sundered for no discernible reason? The grown-ups, who had sobbed so unashamedly as they watched the children marching off dutifully through the streets on the morning of September 1st, now began to question the wisdom of the whole business. Could it be that this vast disruption had been for nothing after all? Then again, surely the bombing raids must become a reality before long? In the meantime, people asked themselves and each other what to do.

In the event, the children prompted their parents to take the matter into their own hands and display one more unpredictable example of the British genius for compromise. The children would agree to go on being evacuated, but not in the holidays. When the first Christmas of the war arrived, thousands of the evacuees returned home joyous at family reunions. Legally there was no restraint on their movements. If they wished to remain evacuees only for part of the time or even not at all, then so be it. There was nothing officialdom could do about it. In the last reckoning the evacuation scheme was a voluntary measure. You could not conscript children. And so the next generation came home for the holidays carrying the same luggage and gas mask it had carried away three months before.

Christmas 1939 proved as bombless as the earlier weeks of the war, and when the festivities were done, back went the evacuees to their havens in the country, back from Glasgow to their Highland fastnesses, from Leeds to Lincolnshire, from Dagenham to Yarmouth, from the East End of London to Wiltshire and Oxfordshire. On December 27th the streets around Waterloo Station saw the children returning to their war postings, their most prominent item of luggage being the cherished Christmas present. But a few of the older evacuees never went back.

In the last weeks of 1939, as the British Expeditionary Force gradually built up its strength, scenes of parting became commonplace. A film-maker posting himself at any London rail terminus could have gathered thousands of feet of love scenes identical to the one featuring the amorous sergeant kissing his lady friend goodbye while a comrade plays smiling goosberry in the carriage behind him. Tin Pan Alley, quick as always to capitalise on the miseries of others, was already offering a wide range of musical tear-jerkers from which departees and their girlfriends could choose. Among the popular songs floating on the air as the sergeant prepares for the peace of battle would be *There'll Always Be an England*, *Blue Skies Are Round the Corner*, *Wish Me Luck As You Wave Me Goodbye*, and the predictable joke-song at the expense of the enemy, the grimly inaccurate *We're Gonna Hang Out the Washing on the Siegfried Line*, which attempted, like the young soldier egged on by his mates, to reduce the pretensions of the enemy to a joke. There was one other popular song this year. It was destined to become the anthem of parting, and, when the war was long finished with, the equally potent anthem of reunion. It was called *We'll Meet Again*, and was the perfect song for the moment, having a melody easy enough to bellowed even in a state of semi-stupor, and the sort of words cunningly calculated to draw crocodile tears from anybody rash enough to think about them. Those who did meet again had a much longer time to wait than anyone could have dreamed as the short, uneventful year of the war ended.

# 1940

The tortuous process by which the British finally arrived at food rationing may amuse those who think they remember rationing being as automatic as the declaration of war itself. For some years before the war, the idea of food rationing had been in the air. And that is where it stayed, in the air. Ration books had been printed, but Mr Chamberlain deferred implementing the scheme for a bizarre reason. He feared that it might panic the nation. However, as the coming of war had appeared to panic nobody apart from the government itself, his reasoning was unwittingly comic. And when the Ministry of Food finally did become operative, it did so from the romantic backwater of Colwyn Bay, a displacement which was part of the government plan whereby, if it could not save the population at large from the consequences of mass bombing, it could a least preserve the civil servants. When the weeks drifted by without the appearance of the bombers, plans to scatter the red tape of the various ministries like confetti across the country were abandoned, but not before the Ministry of Food was despatched to Colwyn Bay and the Admiralty, even more incongruously, to Bath.

Once war began, a great comic contradiction became apparent. The government was unwilling to impose food rationing for fear of panicking a population which was actually demanding it. In the event, the rationing of food caused little hardship throughout the war. What few in government understood was that, for the mass of the population, the rationing of food actually meant more of it and not less. To impose a few ounces per month of butter and meat on a working class which, in the normal way of peacetime things, had never been able to afford either commodity, was to raise, not to lower, the nutritional intake. The paradox arose of a nation embattled and yet better fed than when at peace. The diet was more boring but also more sustaining. One of the contributors was the Ministry of Agriculture, which ploughed up nearly four million acres in the first two years of war, turning the land over to the growing of crops. By 1941 the people of Britain were eating a healthier diet and yet spending twenty per cent less on their food, thanks to the steadily increasing food subsidies.

The photograph of a food shop in 1940 shows how items like jelly, cocoa, custard and tea took the place on the shelves of more exotic items. The pyramid of salmon tins indicates that these are early times in the war; before peace returned, a tin of salmon was regarded as a miracle almost as awesome as a banana. The system by which the ration book holder surrendered points in return for various items worked smoothly enough, but the decision to use the First World War method of linking the customer with a certain retailer probably caused more administrative headaches than it solved.

Once it became clear that, so far as food was concerned, a little less would have to be made to go a little further, the nation began to approach the problem of its own diet with something approaching scientific curiosity. A certain empirical method of husbanding resources began to be more common. By October 1940 Millbank School, located just behind the Tate Gallery in London, had been converted into a part-time feeding centre. What was novel about this type of canteen service was that it was administered by people defined as domestic science experts, a fashionable euphemism for a cook. But the actual cooking, serving and washing-up was all done voluntarily by the teaching staff, which must have lent a certain frisson to the lives of the pupils, now able to ask their tormentors for a cup of tea or a sandwich. Is this the mathematics teacher dispensing bowls of soup at two pence a throw? Or perhaps the gym master, using his finely honed muscles to lift portions of rice pudding singlehanded?

This new experience, of buying prepared food at civic centres, not only stretched the rations a little further but it also turned eating into a social accomplishment. Meals once devoured hastily in purdah now became communal occasions. Another effect of the redisposal of edible resources and the first attempts to place food consumption on a logical basis was quite unforseen by those responsible for implementing it, and even by those who benefited from it. The result of one innovation was to have benign consequences for the health of Britain's children at the expense of its sporting prowess. The effect of the massive injection into the juvenile population of orange juice was to reduce drastically the incidence of stunted, under-developed schoolchildren. Before the war the nation, and particularly industrial Scotland, had produced a long succession of outstanding, tiny professional pugilists who weighed less that eight stone but could hit each other with the force of middleweights. The flyweight division of the professional boxing world was dominated by tiny men like Benny Lynch, Jackie Paterson and Peter Kane. The next generation, exposed to the benefits of vitamin C, grew up healthier and bigger. British domination of the flyweight division passed to the Mexicans and the Japanese, the Indonesians and the Filipinos, none of whom had access either to orange juice or to shepherd's pie with carrots at sixpence a plate.

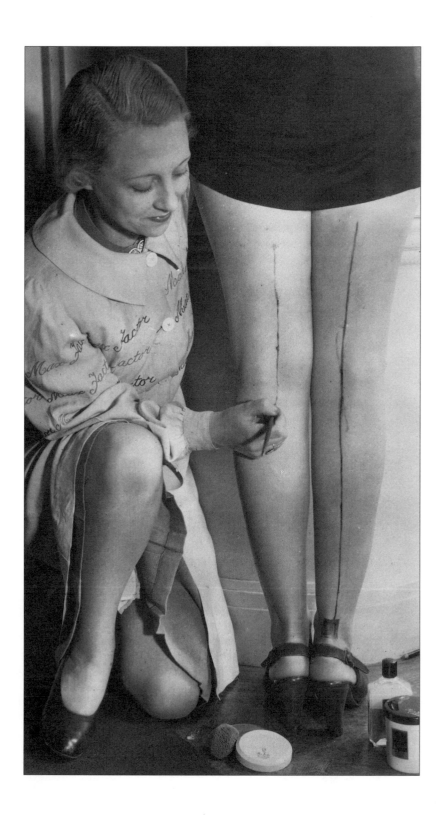

The British young woman's relentless pursuit of glamour was one of the more impressive as well as entertaining aspects of wartime life. The scarcity of silk stockings may have meant little in terms of practical dress, but it was a disastrous setback in the conduct of the battle of the sexes. The silk stocking had come to represent the seamy side of the courting ritual, and at least one film star, the beauteous Madeleine Carroll, had achieved international notoriety by flaunting her silk-stockinged legs in the 1935 production *The Thirty Nine Steps*. With the war, and suddenly deprived of the silk stocking seam which had so flatteringly bisected the back of the legs, the female of the species resorted to the ultimate Carrollian lunacy of a seam without a stocking, which is quite as remarkable as a grin without a cat. The cosmetics expert from Max Factor demonstrates how to achieve this apparent impossibility by the application of a pencil specially designed for the purpose. It may be that the weakmindedness of this sort of behaviour was caused partly by the Spartan wartime diet. The photograph shows the weekly allowance of vital supplies per person in 1940, the same year in which the headless lady is having the backs of her calves disfigured. Meanwhile, the older female of the species is intent on sterner issues, like how to seduce the local butcher. This gloved and bespectacled carnivore is seen indicating the one shilling and fourpenny cut she desires, while the butcher, his ear cleverly separated from his skull by the application of a pencil not specially designed for the purpose, prepares to stab the offending cut of meat to death, performing the considerable music hall feat of wielding a knife in one hand and a ration book in the other.

Although the war started officially on September 3rd, 1939, not till the spring of 1940 did the fighting begin in earnest for the British. The belated removal of Chamberlain in favour of Churchill stirred the nation in its time of grave peril, though some were baffled when Churchill appointed Lord Beaverbrook as Minister of Aircraft Production. Bringing to the making of planes the same sense of dashing melodrama with which he ran his newspapers, Beaverbrook proved a brilliant success, appealing to housewives, 'Send me your pots and pans, send me your aluminium'. The response was instantaneous, but the housewives were soon mystified to see that no sooner had they contributed their cooking utensils than new ones appeared in the shops. By January 1941 the pots-and-pans campaign had yielded a mere 800 tons.

But it had been more of a propaganda exercise than a genuine attempt to stimulate aircraft production. Of little more use was the removal of ironwork from public places. What practical purpose was served by the removal of railings from Victoria Embankment remains unknown, but the scheme did create one of the more lurid legends of the war. When the railings were removed from Astley Hall, the home of Stanley Baldwin, it was said that Beaverbrook was taking his revenge on the retired Prime Minister, who had been his bitter political opponent. There appears to have been no truth in the story, and perhaps more indicative of the natures of the men involved is the fact that Baldwin protested against the requisitioning of his railings even though aware that the country might be able to put them to more practical use.

As the threat of invasion seemed to creep ever closer, preparations were made for a last-ditch battle, among whose most Machiavellian stratagems was the removal of all signposts in the hope of sending enemy columns in the wrong direction. The postwar feeling that the whole business had been a pointless exercise overlooked the fact that the ploy of turning signposts round, only to have them turned back again by some unwitting patriot, was to prove a priceless asset to scriptwriters who were in the business of concocting comedy sequences. By the end of the year, vigilance had been stepped up to the point where even the undergraduates of Emmanuel College, Cambridge, having organised themselves into fire squads, were prepared to swap mortar-boards for steel helmets, don their boots and do their duty.

Even in the extremities of total war, the entrepreneurial genius of the working class continued to flourish. One impromptu caterer, in an unspecified suburb of London, is seen improvising a small but useful income out of the problems of others. Whether the queuing housewives have been deprived of their own facilities for cooking by air raids, or whether their compliance is an attempt to cut down on fuel consumption, or whether all of the people in the photograph are close relations of the photographer who has set it up, remains one of the great unsolved questions of the Second World War.

Whether or not officialdom ever realised it, one of the more frightening recurring nightmares throughout the war was that one night an exploding bomb would release from captivity all the local wild animals, so that the innocent citizen returning home from the air raid shelter in the light of a new morning, having survived all the terrors of the previous night's bombardment, would be waylaid by a marauding horde of wildebeests, Bengal tigers, Barbary apes, anacondas and buffalo. As all dangerous animals from all collections had been removed to the hinterlands at the start of the war, the fears were groundless, unless you happened to be a resident of the hinterlands. When at the height of the Battle of Britain the proprietors of Chapman's Circus removed their two biggest attractions to a Herefordshire farm, the creatures proved so docile that they never even bothered to walk through the flimsy wooden gates which confined them. Locals reported that the poor creatures were intimidated by the swift movements of the farm's rabbits.

The elephants were moving in the wake of the children, who, in a second wave of evacuation at the end of June involving 100,000 infants, were taken from Greater London, some of them for the second time, to safe retreats in the West Country. The photograph illustrates the truth of the hoary cliché that all the nice girls love a sailor.

On September 26th, 1940, two distinguished citizens of London, Jimmy Britnell and his sister Pat, are spotted striding along the platform of one of the capital's great railway termini, en route for a country destination safe from the obscenities of war.

In the ten days previous to the strategic retreat of the Britnells, about 20,000 children had left London in the first large-scale evacuation since the beginning of the Blitz. Life in the country was certainly very different from the sort of hell being endured by London. A fortnight after the Britnells caught their train, ten evacuees enjoy a supervised stroll through a Berkshire village so liberated from the siege conditions in the capital that not one of the eleven pedestrians is encumbered by a gas mask. Behind them on the right stand the sturdy ramparts of 'The Cricketers', while just out of the photograph to their left a poster advertises news which would surely have interested the children, that the Forum Cinema was showing *Pinocchio*. At least one departing Londoner during that month arrived to catch her train prepared for trouble to the very last moment, a tin hat perched on her head. No doubt she returned it to the photographer once the snap was taken.

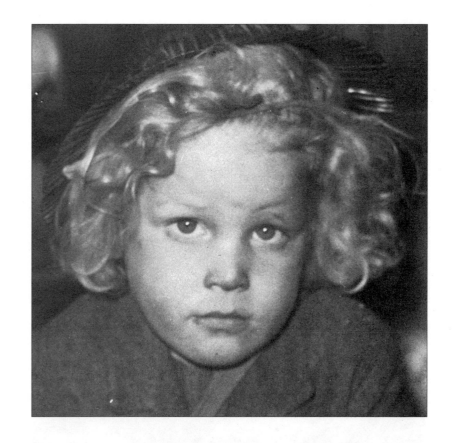

Encroachments on the liberty of the individual did not stop with rationing, the black-out and National Service. All citizens were required to carry with them identity cards which certified that they were not enemy agents or deserters from the armed forces. They were required to show these cards on request at any time, and failure to comply could lead to a fine or even imprisonment. In September 1940, after a bad night in the City of London, people reporting for work at their offices show their cards before being allowed to enter an area so devastated that those offices might no longer be there. At a place called Blaindon, on the outskirts of London, a policeman examines the *bona fides* of a motorcyclist just across the road from the garage run by the Parkinson brothers. Further afield in Surrey in the high summer of the year, the law looks into the affairs of a family of ramblers enjoying the balmy weather. Ramblers were obliged to show not one but two documents, their identity card and the membership card of the ramblers' club to which they were affiliated, which was understandable, as the act of rambling could be the perfect cover for a spy trying to work out whether the signposts which had been turned round had been turned back again. In this case probably the lady's slacks qualify as suspicious objects underneath which a scoundrel might easily secrete a sextant, or a portable radio or a small machine-gun. Most ominous of all is the terrier, patently averse to authority and within an ace of trying a mouthful of policeman's lower leg.

In 1940 the British were still innocent enough about espionage to believe that all people with foreign accents, especially those who had committed the heinous crime of having been born in a foreign land, were potential security risks. And so, while the dashing blades of our own spy system flirted with the idea of betrayal, refugees from the German armies who had fled to Britain were placed under armed guard for the duration. Even in peacetime the refugees had been the subject of much disapproval; by 1939 there were 25,000 of them in Britain, and, to quote Robert Graves and Alan Hodge, 'some of the stupider elements of the Right worked up an agitation against the alleged competition of refugees for jobs which Englishmen could do just as well'. In May 1940, hundreds of aliens were rounded up and packed off to the north of England. Here they were herded onto a new housing estate and placed under armed military surveillance. The housing estate was brand new, but instead of being used for its intended purpose, it was adapted as a ghetto inside which the aliens could be confined. Each home provided accommodation for nine people, and within the camp's perimeter there was complete freedom of movement. On May 21st, the official censor released the sensational news that arrangements were being made for the internees to provide their own concerts and recreations. What sort of concerts and recreations remains speculative, but however they beguiled the long hours it is doubtful if any of them turned to the style of entertainment being advertised in London even as they were being herded up.

It is June 6th, 1940, and a group of women aliens leave their coach to be escorted to a train which will take them to an internment camp 'Somewhere in the North of England'. Behind them are indications of the way Britain reacts to the treachery of real enemy agents, by making a joke of them. The radio buffoon known as Lord Haw-Haw was much in the news, and the butt of half the comedians in the country. The impresario George Black opened a new revue in December 1940 at the ill-fated Holborn Empire, and kept it running until July of the following summer. But the revue was not an unqualified success despite its star, Max Miller, the nation's most accomplished comic and the very personification of cockney London, even though Miller was a Brightonian. He was supreme as a stand-up comic delivering a stream of patter bubbling with innuendo. But in *Haw-Haw* he was obliged to exchange dialogue with other members of the cast, a foolish idea ruinous to his cause. Miller did what he could to counter the obtuseness of his producer, but to give him character roles in sketches was not the best way of bringing out his genius. In one scene he portrayed an old soldier. In another sketch he impersonated Hitler. Of the rest of the cast, Ben Lyon and Bebe Daniels were a husband-and-wife team who had once been Hollywood stars but were now happy to be among the more popular duets in British showbusiness. Their style was more genteel than Miller's and much, much less entertaining. Without question the most prolific source of laughter in *Haw-Haw* apart from Miller would have been Syd Seymour, who was to musicmaking what Billy Bennett was to the English language. Also featured in the show was Gaston Palmer, a juggler who deliberately dropped everything he juggled with, and a troupe of can-can girls to take the mind of the tired businessman off the war. Curiously the period was a prolific one for revue in London's West End. Flanagan and Allen had starred in *The Little Dog Laughed* in the first Christmas of the war, and introduced a song related to the fact that rabbits were not rationed: *Run, Rabbit, Run*.

At the London Hippodrome in that first wartime winter Pat Kirkwood made her reputation with *My Heart Belongs to Daddy* in *Black Velvet*, while down the street at the Princes the revue *Shepherd's Pie* introduced one of the big hits of the war, *Who's Taking You Home Tonight*. At the Savoy in February 1940 the blonde American Evelyn Dall was drawing the town with *You've Done Something To My Heart*, and in August 1940, after the end of the run of *Haw Haw*, a new show opened at the Holborn Empire called *Apple Sauce*, again starring Miller, whose favourite theatre it had always been. One of his fellow-artists, Doris Hare, recalled, 'I remember the stage doorkeeper at the Holborn Empire used to stand outside and watch the bombs dropping in distant parts of London. One night a bomb dropped on the theatre, and we closed prematurely'. And forever. The Holborn Empire never reopened, but was demolished to make way for some tiresome modern improvement.

By the summer of 1940 Britain was dotted with observation posts manned by part-time civilians who charted the height and course of enemy bombers and then telephoned the nearest RAF fighter station to tip them off. Some of these posts were on the roofs of buildings, others along the coastline, still others at any point likely to attract the enemy. Railways and docks were specially pinpointed targets and the vigil continued round the clock. Perhaps the most bizarre observation post was the one on the roof of the United States Embassy, created on the order of the Ambassador and manned by members of the diplomatic staff. The photograph shows three gentlemen so immaculately dressed that for them spending ration points on clothes is clearly an unknown experience. The gentleman at the centre of operations is Mr James Seymour, a graduate of Harvard University and the unit's chief spotter. The man dangling his legs over the precipice is Major McDonald, the head man of the embassy ARP. The photograph was taken in September 1940 and, taking into account the nicety that the embassy building was technically United States territory, the observation post on the roof may well have been a breach of neutrality.

When at last London was subjected to nightly attempts to wipe it off the map, the population, seeing that the government had made hopelessly inadequate provisions for those who wished to take shelter, took matters into its own hands and improvised in typically English style. Fortunately for the town, it was provided with the most comprehensive underground railway system in the world. Most of the stations were deep enough to offer virtual immunity from the bombers, and almost before the authorities knew what was happening, the London underground railway stations of 'The Tube' were virtually commandeered. An uncanny nightlife began to flourish, a life undreamed-of by the pioneers who had designed and built the system. At station after station across the metropolis, a sizeable proportion of Londoners retired for the night, taking with them bedding, food and clothing, books and newspapers, pyjamas and dressing gowns. They slept on the platforms, sometimes in bunks, sometimes on the ground. Tiny townships came into being, each with a fierce pride in its spirit of community. The ritual began early in the evening, when the smaller children were bedded down for the night, their slumbers interrupted by the constant periodic crash and roar of trains stopping and starting. Other towns, less fortunate, made do with the natural features of the landscape. The fugitives huddled in their cave, smiling at the camera while a little girl is prevailed upon to swallow something from a cup, are residents of Ramsgate, a town, which, the moment the air war over Britain began in earnest, became a front-line town, one of the first tempting targets to attract the enemy squadrons crossing the English Channel.

For the troglodytes of the London Tube, life quickly settled into new patterns. Makeshift catering arrangements ensured that people had neither to venture upstairs into danger to feed themselves, nor to stay below and go hungry. The lady bountiful carrying a basket of edibles is a voluntary worker whose tariff is as moderate as good housekeeping allows. The packet of biscuits she is handing to a small child costs two pence; for the same price the kid could have had a bar of chocolate. Apples started the day at two pence, but have now been reduced to three-halfpence. The diet is nutritional but Spartan, and would hardly attract the City gent stranded at Aldwych by an air raid. A double Scotch would be more in his line, and in its absence he snoozes on the platform, his hat serving as an eyeshade, his pinstriped trousers hauled up for comfort. The edition of *The Evening News* lying at his side tells that the Battle of Britain is at its height, and that it is beginning to dawn on the beleaguered British that they are about to enjoy their first major victory of the war. The *Luftwaffe* is being knocked to pieces, and the prospect of invasion receding steadily. Meanwhile the gentleman on the platform snoozes on in comparitive peace. Later that night sleep would not be so easy to come by. Once the last train has gone through, the power is switched off and the lines running through Aldwych become the pit of a makeshift theatre, with the platform serving as a stage. ENSA was quick to provide distraction for the sheltering thousands, among whom only the intensely musical preferred the threat of bombs to the torment of wrong harmonies.

Safety is not always the first consideration. The warmth of your own bed, especially when central heating is supplied free of charge by the adjacency of your own kith and kin, is sometimes sweeter than life itself, and there were countless millions who gradually acquired the courage, or the fatalism, to ignore the air-raid sirens, spurn the shelters, and sleep on at home. These four of life's apprentices slumber on, blissfully oblivious to the fact that outside in the streets history is being made. Survival, they seem to be implying, is as much a matter of luck as of judgement, in which conclusion they will often be justified by events. One night in southeast London a landmine fell on the local tennis court. The local warden, examining the crater, found a second, delayed-action bomb a few feet from the crater. He immediately cleared the residents from the local houses and shelters. A few hours later the bomb exploded, on the morning of September 21st, 1940. Later that day the evacuated residents returned and exulted in the narrowness of their escape by posing in and on the flimsy shelter which would have offered little protection had not that warden saved the day. Providential escapes of this kind became part of the daily routine of London life in 1940, and people leaned against the counters of a thousand saloon bars murmuring sagely that if it had your name on it ....

One of the few welcome effects of total war is that it gives the female of the species a chance to show that she is not merely decorative and otherwise useless. It is one of the ironies of English history that while the Suffragettes of Edwardian Britain underwent all sorts of brutality in their struggle for the vote and achieved little of practical use, the moment the 1914-18 war started, women were recruited in their tens of thousands to the war effort, performing with such efficiency that, once peace returned, any further arguments against their suitability as voters were confined to the mentally inept. In the second war they served once more, and performed vital services in key industries. The ladies in the quaintly antiquated mobcaps are manufacturing ammunition of an unspecified nature. The work was hard, the uniforms unbecoming.

Compared to them, the girls of the Land Army were positively glamorous. When the farmer went to war, he left behind fields to till, seeds to sow, harvests to gather. Women took over much of the drudgery of the job, and more than one English landscape was animated by the stride of the suntanned Amazon carrying hay or carting potatoes. These two young ladies are the sisters Hewer, who have run their Kentish farm for fifteen years, and have now contributed to the war effort by digging up the pot-pourri and pomander flowers of peace, so that they can cultivate aconite for use in the manufacture of medical drugs.

### 'SOCIETY NOTES'

Mrs Fellowes-Gordon, of Knockespoch, Aberdeenshire, seen here at the wheel of an emergency ambulance, is a cousin of the United States President, Franklin D. Roosevelt. While her husband is away on active service, Mrs Fellowes-Gordon devotes much time and energy to the supervision of an ambulance unit in St. Pancras. Her links with the White House are further strengthened by the fact that Mr Roosevelt is her godfather, and sends her a congratulatory letter each year on her birthday. Mrs Fellowes-Gordon has done a great deal to establish the fashion of wearing a steel helmet with a string of pearls, and is in addition so well connected in the motor trade that she is able to procure ambulances of the type she prefers driving at the bargain price of two shillings and sixpence a dozen.

Night after night the rain of fire-bombs falling on London was reflected for miles around in the dull magenta glow of the sky. In the City of London whole areas were razed, and on such occasions the war suddenly became a fight between an air force and a fire brigade. The fire-fighting services of London, from the London Fire Brigade to the most modest auxiliaries, performed prodigious feats of valour. Likely to be blown up by a bomb at any moment, or buried under an avalanche of molten masonry, or asphyxiated by the poisoned air, or burnt alive, or flung to certain death from ladders collapsing in the inferno, the firemen numbered among the great heroes of the war. And very often, lingering in the shadows just behind them were the official photographers, courting dangers almost as frightful in their attempts to record the war even as it was being fought. The result of their labours was a terrible beauty, a series of images at once aesthetically perfect and hideous in their import.

The profile of the London skyline, with one lone waterspout contending against acres of flame, is one of the most brilliant images of the war, with St Paul's Cathedral miraculously avoiding disaster, and on the left the geometric loveliness of the church of St Mary le Bow. In 1941 this church was engulfed by the flames of a new fire, and it was not until 1956 that restoration was begun. The ironies of total war are reflected in the cameo of three members of the Auxiliary Fire Service aiming their waterjet high in the air, while within feet of the flames stands a board advertising 'Offices to Let'.

The British have always sung throughout their wars. At home the message is usually sentimental, at the front a deal more Rabelaisian. In 1914-18 they kept insisting it was a long way to Tipperary and that under the circumstances the best thing to do was to pack up your troubles in your old kit-bag and smile. Men returning from the Somme would attend a performance of *The Bing Boys*, wallow in *If You Were the Only Girl in the World* and sob quietly to themselves. In the second war the items ranged from the pastoral absurdity of *There'll Always Be an England* to the facetiousness of Tommy Handley making jokes about Hitler. The revue writer Herbert Farjeon even suggested that Hitler must have had a mother, and another popular song, its title borrowed from a poorish J. B. Priestley novel, gave as its war-winning policy, *Let the People Sing*.

On the morning of September 27th, 1940, in the aftermath of an air raid, the George Formby song, W*hen I'm Cleaning Windows*, takes on a new meaning, but the odd process by which songwriters may steal each other's titles without fear of litigation makes it impossible to be precise about the other items on display. *Who Cares* may be the Gershwin song from 1930, but it may well be a later, less distinguished piece. As for the item immediately below it, there lies a riddle indeed. There is an excellent song called *Gone With the Wind* which has no connection with the film of that name. Yet the song is advertised with a sketch of Rhett Butler and Scarlett O'Hara. But there was no song called *Gone With the Wind* in the film *Gone With the Wind*. Anyone buying the song copy would probably have found himself landed with *Tara's Theme*. In any case, the milkman showing that it was 'business as usual' would have been whistling none of these songs, but would have much preferred *We'll Meet Again*, or *We're Gonna Hang Out the Washing on the Siegfried Line*.

Somewhere in London, September 9th, 1940, morning. Last night a gangster dropped a bomb on an obscure community, smashing its life to pieces in the name of some fine cause or other. Some of the houses in the terrace have vanished; others have been lucky only to lose their front doors, have their windows blown out, their roofs riddled, their occupants' pathetic possessions destroyed. The inhabitants are doing what they can to salvage what they can of the lives which ended a few hours ago. A child's cot, a sprung bed frame but no bed, a few books piled on a small table, and in the gutter a dusty upright piano, now more than ever in need of tuning. Some picture frames, a chair standing on its head like truth itself, a cushion, a box, a drawer from a missing chest. The rescue men work away; one of them questions a local inhabitant. On the pavement a young man is in earnest conversation with a nun whose crisply-starched wimple makes a stark, snow-white contrast to everything else in evidence. And in the foreground a quartet of matriarchs trying to make some sort of sense out of what is perfectly senseless.

Mr Charles Rolfe and his wife Elizabeth were both born in 1864 into a world not yet clever enough to know how to blow old people into the street. Wearied of their ordeal, they sleep fitfully in the September sun, surrounded by the wreckage of their home. Her arthritic fingers and lace-up boots, his tightly-buttoned jacket and faded scarf, the trilby and the bonnet, the chortling walrus moustache of the one, the imitation fur collar and cuffs of the other, tell more of 1940 than a library of books. One of the great portraits of 1939-45. Total war. And did you, Charles Rolfe and your wife Elizabeth live to see the end of it?

The remarkable illustration showing that half a flag is better than none was taken in London at the height of the Blitz, in September 1940, after the effects of an air raid had included the sundering of the Union Jack. And in one of the nearby devastated streets, four small boys improvise. By flinging ropes about the truncated stem of a blasted corporation lamppost, they whirl round, back across the centuries to a time when the maypole was a commonplace of daily life.

Throughout the war the common people never lost their sense of incredulity at the sheer presumption of the dictators, an emotion which received its expression in a million ways as the fighting went on. Towards the end of November, armoured against the approaching winter with their overcoats, a cluster of Londoners queue for apples at three pence a pound, oranges at five pence. That already sybaritic luxury, the banana, dangles from the roof of the stall. It is a certainty that each customer will be allowed only one. There is no street, only rubble, no life, only chaos, no community, only deprivation and destruction. Yet the stall-owner still possesses the detachment of risible comment. His hoarding makes sarcastic reference to the fact that British ships continue to sail through a sea which Mussolini liked to think of as his own. The engraving on the side of the stall tells that the fruiterer and his wife come from the parish of St George's, in the heart of the East End.

And what of the postman? Condemned to trudge every morning through the wreckage of last night's raid, expected to deliver letters to addresses which no longer exist, he does what he can, like the milkman and the paperboy, to foster the illusion that life continues. It would be interesting to show the photograph of the postman making his collection to Anthony Trollope, who wrote millions of words, many of them about Barsetshire, but whose lasting monument is his invention of the pillar-box. The photographic evidence suggests that in the event of an air raid the safest thing to do was to post yourself in the nearest available letterbox, for it certainly looks as if it alone stands while all about it crumbles. But who are the obdurate believers who, when their district has been levelled, still have the time to write a letter, still have the faith to post it? And what does the postman do when he arrives with a letter only to find that the letterbox has vanished, along with the rest of the front door? He writes what details he can on the envelope and returns it to the depot, which will do what it can to find the addressee.

On October 28th, 1940, a London orphanage is blown out of its premises. A cotted survivor takes stock of the landscape. Is this what the grown-ups consider to be a good thing? The small boy on his tricycle pauses for a moment on his journey to study that funny zigzag space between the bricks on that wall over there. What fun.

The pavement is spangled with fragments of broken glass. In the aftermath of the bombs, a young man with head wounds is given moral support by two policemen and a member of Civil Defence. Considering that he is cut about the head and face, the young man displays surprising awareness that his photograph is being taken. His composure is particularly underlined by the soigné style with which he brandishes the lit cigarette which those who patched up his head supplied. He will recover. Not so the great, ancient buildings of London which were lost to the aerial war. Among the irreparable losses is Staple Inn, once the centre of the wool trade, where wool was weighed and duties paid on it. The Elizabethan Hall, one of the finest surviving examples of the architecture of the period, was destroyed by a landmine.

The man in the wheelchair is a veteran of the British Expeditionary Force. He was wounded in the fighting in France, and has not seen his two small daughters since he left England. Today is June 8th, 1940. At hospitals all over the country it is visiting day, and the two small girls, white-socked and beribboned, run into the wounded man's arms. The caption accompanying the photograph was 'Hello Daddy', which sounds like an excess of sentimentality. But in war everything sounds like an excess of everything.

# 1941

By the start of 1941, the British were a nation under siege, the only effective force left to oppose Germany. Her allies had quickly succumbed, leaving the nation isolated. There had been victories in 1940, especially the combination of the Spitfire and Hurricane squadrons under the command of Hugh Dowding, and the profound strategic advantage which came with the fortuitous possession of radar, which frustrated enemy attempts to clear the skies over the English Channel in preparation for invasion. The nightly bombing raids, an attempt to break the spirit of the civilian population, had, by the end of 1940, shown no sign of achieving its ends; indeed, its effect could be seen as negative, in the sense that it appeared to have stiffened the resistance of the victims. The resource, common sense, stoicism and bloody-minded courage of the British throughout this period became the wonder of the world, which looked on in awe as the battering went on and the British continued to make jokes about it even as they fought grimly on. It was the reaction that buttressed the belief of Americans like the humorist Frank Sullivan, who wrote to the *New Yorker* editorial assistant E.B. White in August 1940, saying 'I'm confident that England can't be licked'.

Such opinions were more sentimental than logical, but they proved to be justified. All previous experience of the mass bombing of large cities had suggested that there could be only one conclusion; the disarray of the population and the collapse of vital services. In a city of eight million, like London, deaths might reach into six or even seven figures. In the event, the Blitz killed 30,000 people, half of them Londoners. The appropriation by Londoners of the underground system as a makeshift but perfectly effective sheltering device was one example of how to bear the unbearable. Another was the ploy of the mass exodus. Once Plymouth had suffered its first heavy night raid, 50,000 residents decamped for the surrounding countryside each night, returning the next morning to pick up the threads. London seemed more indifferent to danger; even at the height of the bombing, six locals out of ten slept at home. Deeds of valour became so commonplace that in September a new decoration, the George Cross, was instituted for acts of civil bravery.

Amidst the inferno, the miraculous thing was that one of the largest and most easily identifiable buildings in Britain remained unharmed. The dome of St Paul's Cathedral loomed over the ravaged streets like a mystical presence. That it and the great clock tower of Big Ben should have survived the bombing may not have been much of a strategic asset, but in psychological terms they counted as huge victories. Other ancient aspects of the town were less fortunate, and among the casualties was the Temple, the heartland of legal life, which, as the new year dawned, required some vital evidence to be provided by the Fire Brigade.

This photograph of the premises of *The Times* newspaper surely ranks among the most ironic of the entire war. Throughout the 1930s, down to the very eve of the declaration of war and even beyond it, *The Times* had pursued a pro-German policy, politely defined as 'Appeasement'. Its editor, one Geoffrey Dawson, cooked the news, misled his readers, and turned the paper into a virtual propaganda arm of the German government. The surprise is contained not in Dawson's fatuous intellectual dishonesty, but in his presence as editor at all. He had been a product of 'Milner's Kindergarten' in South Africa a generation before, and, ethically speaking, a kindergarten remained his natural habitat for the rest of his life. His training under Milner had left him so pro-German that in 1919 he had been sacked as editor by Lord Northcliffe, who said of him, 'Dawson is naturally pro-German. He just can't help it'. Lord Astor's first move on acquiring the paper had been to reinstate Dawson, with what calamitous results everyone now knows. The editorial for September 7th, 1938, praising the dismemberment of Czechoslovakia for the convenience of Hitler, was written by Dawson personally. It would have been poetic justice had someone required him to write a second editorial for the edition of October 4th, 1941. On approaching *The Times* building that morning en route to his place of work, he would have been confronted by the scene shown in the photograph. Rarely has any fool seen his theories crumble into rubble as literally as this.

Among the many millions of Dawson's time who were not quite sophisticated enough to see his point of view was the rescue worker who spent part of February 27th, 1941, burrowing under the wreckage of a bombed London house in an attempt to reach a trapped occupant.

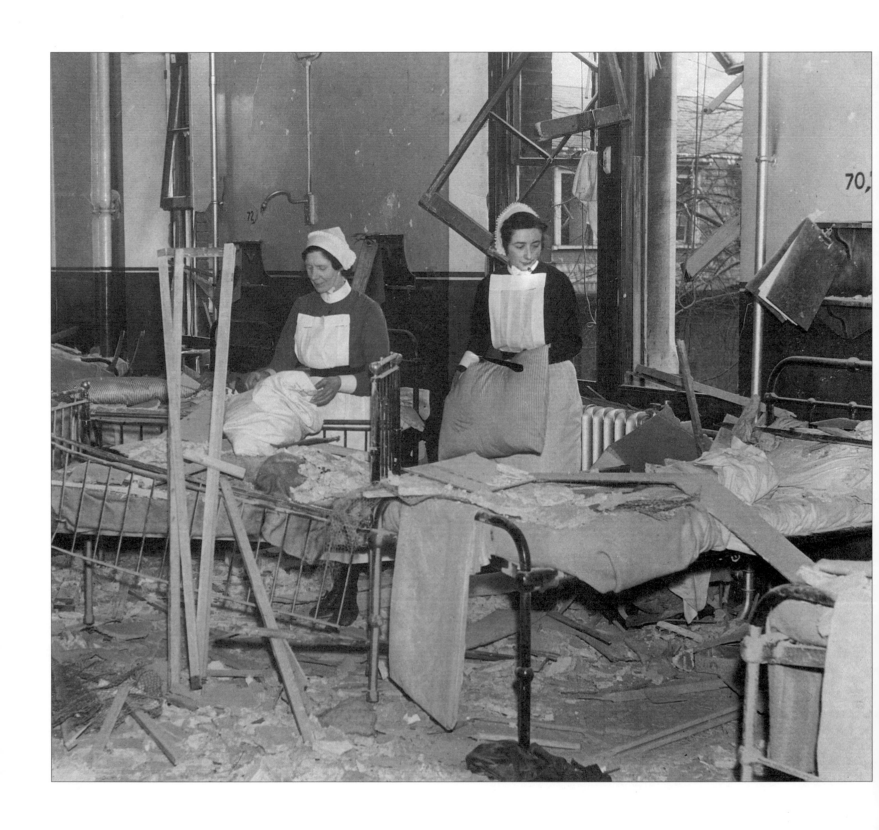

The ways of censorship were something peculiar. Torn between a desire to publicise the barbarism of the enemy to the rest of the world, and an equally keen desire not to tell anyone exactly what had been damaged, the official censor would release photographs like these without being specific as to their location, even though anyone who cared to take the trouble could have pinpointed their whereabouts without much trouble. The hospital ward smashed by bombing was defined as 'somewhere in London', March 21st. A month earlier, the photograph of rescue workers helping a nurse tend a wounded man was a little more forthcoming. On the night of February 26th, a London ARP post had suffered a direct hit, after which an all-night search had been made by survivors for colleagues buried under the rubble. The picture shows a warden holding bandages while one of his colleagues takes a pick to the task of removing some of the debris But the photograph, which appeared in a long-vanished print called *The News Chronicle*, made identification simple enough by naming the nurse, Sister Dorothy Hall.

The twists and turns of political fortune might have been comic had they not been concerned with events so tragic. It is worth recalling that on the eve of the outbreak of the Second World War, Germany and the Soviet Union astounded themselves and each other by signing a pact whereby the Soviet Union agreed to remain neutral should Germany find itself involved in war, which removed, at least on paper, the German terror of being caught in a war on two fronts. One effect of this bizarre alliance was that all committed communists believed it their duty to oppose the war against Germany, because, since the pact, a war against Germany might be construed as a war against the Soviet Union, which most communists deluded themselves into believing would be a war against the cause of socialism. The organ of the British Communist Party was *The Daily Worker*, a strident partisan sheet catering to the dreams of a tiny minority of true believers. Throughout the first fifteen months of the war, *The Daily Worker* pursued an editorial policy of opposition to the war, which was not surprising. There were those, including Herbert Morrison, the Home Secretary, who believed that these editorial squeaks constituted a threat to national morale, which was very surprising indeed. How little effect the anti-war campaign was having is reflected in the events of December 1940, when the members of the Independent Labour Party in the House of Commons proposed a motion for a negotiated peace. It lost the vote by 341-4. A month later *The Daily Worker* summoned something called a 'People's Convention', which, under the guise of being a plea for better air-raid shelters, attempted further agitation against the war. The Home Secretary then banned the paper from being published, thereby doing the British Communist Party the great service of saving it from its own folly. By banning its appearance, Morrison was preventing the *The Daily Worker* from placing itself in the idiotic position of campaigning against a war which, on June 22nd 1941, when Hitler invaded the Soviet Union, suddenly became a holy crusade.

On January 21st, 1941, a motorised column consisting of nineteen detectives arrived at the offices of *The Daily Worker* in Cayton Street, EC. The photograph shows how few policemen were considered sufficient to hold off protesters against the closure.

One of the problems of life in wartime London was a genuine novelty for the vast bulk of the population: how to spend your money. One of the effects of rationing had been an appreciable drop in private spending, and social historians will not find it difficult to evolve theories from the list of the only four items on which the population at large was spending more money, not less: beer, cigarettes, the cinema and public transport. By 1941 personal consumption was down by fourteen per cent, which proved to be a godsend for the Chancellor of the Exchequer, a bespectacled ex-insurance dullard called Kingsley Wood, one of the very few members of Chamberlain's appeasement brigade to survive into Churchill's cabinet. Wood's problem was how to find the extra five hundred million pounds which was calculated to be the annual gap between what the government was collecting in taxes and what it was spending on the war. Wood raised part of the deficit by increasing the basic rate of income tax to ten shillings in the pound. The rest he hoped in a vague sort of way might come from personal savings. After all, that missing fourteen per cent had to go somewhere, so why not to fund the government? Although the accent on savings brought a firm, patriotic response, it never quite closed the gap between income and expenditure, although it did go a long way towards making Wood's position tenable. In May 1941, London launched its War Savings Week, a campaign which entailed a certain outlay on hoardings with which to deface Nelson's Column. The tiny advertising plaque in the lower right-hand corner of the plinth, 'Harris does it again', proclaims the fact that the same gentleman who had plastered the column with savings posters in the First World War was doing it again in the Second.

The struggle for money to fund the conduct of the war quickly became personalised in the features of the opposing war leaders, each of whom possessed the sort of features which were caricatured easily enough. Churchill's billycock and his cigar clamped in a bulldog jaw became the symbol of a sort of latterday John Bull, while Hitler's apology for a moustache, beloved of a thousand comedians, and the lock of combed-down hair said to conceal a forehead with a one-in-six gradient, was taken to be a joke at the expense of the 'Blond Aryan' theory he propagated. These two cartoon characters were often opposed in patriotic advertising. In February 1941, pupils of the Sydney Cook School in Canterbury do for Westgate Tower what Mr Harris and company was soon to do for Nelson. Canterbury's Weapons Week was staged in the last week of February, and was no less successful than any other. Its preferred effigy was of the nation's war leader, under whose feet was printed one of his most famous slogans, originally addressed to neutral America. After the war, the tens of thousands of schoolboys obliged to waste endless hours in the school woodwork shop without acquiring anything vaguely resembling a skill, perverted the slogan to read, 'Give us the job and we will finish the tools'. Meanwhile, the Deputy Mayor of Tewkesbury unveiled a portrait of the enemy at the local Town Hall, the idea being that by contributing £1,000, the locals could fill in one of the forty squares in the poster; by contributing £40,000, they could obliterate the portrait entirely. Some excuse for the complexity of the joke is provided by the fact that the Deputy Mayor performed the unveiling ceremony on April 1st.

One of the more daring innovations in British life during the war has been generally forgotten. When in 1941 it became apparent that the great bugbear was manpower, the government vastly increased its potential resources at the stroke of a pen by making Great Britain the first of the belligerents and, as it proved, the only one, to introduce conscription for women. Nobody objected. On the contrary, people seemed so willing to serve that tens of thousands of women rushed to do what they could. The three earnest young Amazons directing the powerful water jet are fire-fighting volunteers, devoting all their leisure time to the acquirement of those techniques necessary to fight fire in the event of a resumption of the Blitz. Already they have become adept in the technique of directing the jets while wearing masks to protect them from fumes and smoke, and can, in the words of the original caption, 'shin up a ladder with the expertise of steeplejacks'.

Women undertook maintenance work of every description, and certainly gave the railway services a brighter, friendlier look. The dropiscal porter of pre-war days was in thousands of cases replaced by some trim young lady who, having once been a passenger herself, had some idea of the sort of minor courtesies which make a customer feel at home. With the male staff of the railways away in uniform, the ladies were required to keep the stations looking as trim as themselves. At the Southern Railway Station of Dunton Green, a pair of odd-job ladies, each handicapped by a hat of unusually repellant aspect, take part in a carefully posed photograph to show that the female of the species is perfectly capable of mucking about with spanners and paint brushes when the times demand it.

Life on the London buses was also transformed by the replacement of male conductors with their female counterparts. The lady conductors were especially ingenious in the art of complying with the regulations applying to the wearing of uniforms while making themselves up to look like film stars, or at any rate recognisable imitations of film stars. This was particularly noticeable in the way hundreds of them were able to sport a Betty Grable perm or a Dorothy Lamour arrangement while wearing the peaked cap which came with the job. By judicious use of pins and clips, the cap could be made very nearly to disappear, the resulting effect being so ravishing that more than one young male would take the wrong bus to the wrong destination in the hope of finding the special conductress who twanged his callow heartstrings.

It is very likely that many of the women who flinched in their shelters at the crump of the anti-aircraft batteries were the same women who earlier in the day had been working to produce the very shells now exploding above their kitchen roofs. All over Britain empty industrial premises were being converted into miniature munitions factories. The lady with legs like fine English oaks, pushing a trolley of projectiles into an oven to be dried after lacquering, is working in premises which until recently had been a service garage. Only a year ago she may have been a typist busily producing bumph in triplicate, or a shop asistant, or even a tweenie in some draughty hall. But whatever she had been, the odds were strongly against her returning to the old ways once the war was over. The lives of millions of Britain's women were transformed by the experience of performing war duties.

Perhaps as they went about their new work the ladies paused sometimes and shook their capped heads in bewilderment at the wonderland politics of so-called adult men. On June 21st, 1941, Russia was a sinister neutral power, tied by treaty to the enemy. A day later she was our glorious ally. Hitler, committing the key strategic blunder of his life, suddenly invaded his ally, choosing the same day for his fatal enterprise as had Napoleon Bonaparte more than a century before. His expedition was to end as well as begin in Napoleonic style. For the moment the ladies of the munitions factories dutifully obeyed the edict of the Minister of Supply, Lord Beaverbrook, who told them that the Soviet army was 'fighting in the same just cause as our own'. By the middle of September, 1941, with Moscow under seige, the ladies have already acquired the linguistic skill to scrawl on their tanks 'Greetings to our Allies' in two languages.

The battle to feed the guns was desperate enough, but even more vital the struggle to feed the people. In every county the arcane arts of husbandry suddenly became the study of thousands of women who combined a love of the countryside, the stimulus of fresh air and a sense of patriotic obligation by toiling through the day with hoes, rakes and shovels. In the Vale of Evesham, one of England's most renowned beauty spots, dubbed The Garden of England, a lone lady strives to convert it into the Market Garden of England, She is performing the act known as intercropping, whereby the ground separating rows of vegetables is utilised in another way. This worker is preparing the precious spaces between rows of peas for planting with radishes. The Women's Land Army was often assisted by eager holidaymaking schoolchildren. In Oakwood Park, Southgate, the youngsters frolic in the August sun and describe it all as helping to bind the corn. Sterner work is afoot at Hornchurch, where the patriots of Drury Falls Council School march off to war work which is showing a tidy profit. The produce from their two-and-a-half-acre allotment is sold to parents, and the proceeds shared by the workers in National Savings stamps.

Sometimes the intrepid townie, daring to poke his nose over the parapet after the warning sirens have sounded, is rewarded for his curiosity with the spectacle of the old familiar world transformed. The slender swords of light reach up to the roof of high clouds, probing the skies, hoping to converge on a lone raider who might then present a more reasonable target to the anti-aircraft gunners. The searchlight beam is one of the most spectacular stage effects of the war, often mingling with the dull glow of fires, but usually, as in this remarkable picture, forming a brilliant, flashing, shifting mesh, slicing up the blackness of the night sky.

The art of policing the skies at night was a difficult one to acquire, and the only effective training was to practice under battle conditions. The glimpse of seven artillerymen firing their gun may look authentic enough, but appearances in propaganda photographs can be misleading. In fact the men are recruits at a Southern Command Artillery School, learning how the damn thing works. But the six men here gratefully wolfing an improvised alfresco breakfast, have been doing the real thing. It is early morning in central London, 1941, and the gunners have spent the night beating back the enemy squadrons. Whatever is in the sandwiches, it is welcome, although artilleryman number two seems to be prodding his into submission, while number six has that look about him of an eager diner who has just bitten on a bad tooth.

The ironies of war occasionally became patent in terrible ways. The anti-aircraft batteries defending the skies over the great cities occasionally scored a bullseye with results just as grievous as a clutch of exploding bombs. On the morning of April 17th, 1941, the residents of a London suburb rose from their beds to find the army standing guard over a patch of desolation which literally looks as though a bomb has hit it. In fact, what has happened is that a bomber has hit it. For once the debris constitutes a deathly melange of the military and the domestic. An enemy bomber has crashed to its end on to a London street, and the evidence has about it a touch of the allegorical: a propeller blade, German, lying alongside a section of blasted drainpipe, British; a section of shattered wing, German, next to a chair leg, British. The plane wreckage would be examined by men from the Air Ministry and then carted away for scrap, perhaps to be melted down into more of the shells which brought about the crash. But what of the Londoners who lost their lives, or at the very least their homes, through the impact? They must have had mixed feelings about the accuracy of our gunners. A month later, on May 9th, a censor released a picture showing three soldiers guarding the shattered remains of a Junkers 88 bomber which had come to grief just outside London, fortunately for the local residents, in a nearby park. Two of the soldiers examine some enemy bullets, while a third stands guard. In the distance, two curious onlookers watch, standing on grass scattered with fragments of the wrecked plane.

Whenever an enemy plane was brought down, some of its crew might survive the crash to be taken prisoner. According to the rules of the game, combatants thus captured were interrogated and then interned for the duration. For the captured air crews the war was well and truly over, just as it was for the thirty thousand civilians who died at their hands during the Blitz. After the war there was much talk among fliers of the cameraderie of the air which superseded causes and nations to form a brotherhood of heroes, but it is hard to see what was heroic about dropping bombs on old ladies. This young German failure looks happy enough as the realisation dawns upon him that his duties are suspended, at least for the moment. Many prisoners of war were put to work on the land; a few, once the war was over, married local girls and stayed in the country of their captivity. At least one settled down in Manchester and became a local, and then a national hero. Private Trautmann, ex-prisoner of war, resumed his pre-war footballing wars and eventually earned a trial as goalkeeper with Manchester City. Soon he was in the League side and in 1955 went to Wembley with the side that was defeated 3-1 by Newcastle United. In the following year Manchester City won their way through to the Cup Final once again, and this time Trautmann was not only on the winning side, against Birmingham City, but became a front-page hero when it was discovered that the daring, full-length dive at an opponent's feet which saved an almost certain goal, had broken his neck. In spite of the injury, Trautmann played on to the end of the game, without question the most admirable piece of behaviour by any member of any branch of the German armed forces.

But not all German prisoners of war found their way into the Manchester City side. In March 1941 travellers on one of the great London railway routes might have caught a closer glimpse than usual of the enemy. Three captured German airmen, one with a Hitler moustache, another still wearing his flying boots, march along a platform whose edge is decorated inevitably with the white stripe of the war. The armed escort is taking them to an internment camp somewhere in England, where they will sit out the rest of the war, still more than four years away. A few weeks earlier, two of their fellow bombers had passed through the same station, presenting a touching cameo of the freemasonry of the military life. The young captured pilot, whose list of battle honours must by this time have numbered countless old ladies and children, gives a piggyback ride to his injured observer, who is further supported by the friendly assistance and broad shoulders of a British Military Policeman. The police sergeant on the right of the picture offers a memorable example of the ways in which the British contrived even in their darkest hour to keep a stiff upper lip.

The idea that any woman could possibly find her way around any piece of machinery was one which the male population received with its customary boneheaded hilarity. Even when the war was under way and thousands of women were serving as drivers and mechanics, the suspicion continued to smoulder in many a male chauvinist breast that the whole thing was a bad joke. One woman later recalled that when she started taking classes in engine maintenance, the idea of a female mechanic seemed revolutionary. Throughout her course, the instructors poured scorn and ridicule upon her even though she proved proficient. And later, when the class was moved into the workshop, only two of the women proved strong enough to resist the scorn flung at them by their male fellow workers. Among the other facts about 'the woman in war' which were all-too-rarely publicised was the disgraceful victimisation of female workers through the instrument of the wage-packet. Women's wages were much lower than those of men performing identical duties, a corruption of justice which fifty years later could still be found in most industries. Another fact which was smudged away in the furore of patriotism of the time was the disparity between the recruiting publicity and the reality. The three members of the Auxiliary Territorial Service seen here competing in motor cycle trials were among the fortunate few for whom some vestiges of excitement did attach to the job, although at least one of the men in the background seems to be enjoying the old joke about women drivers.

In September 1941 the Port of London Authority was busily rehearsing its Home Guard units in the art of climbing up and down the walls of the docks, a practice which was, according to the caption, 'among the most effective ways of dealing with the enemy'.

Sometimes the official mind moved so slowly that hardly any movement could be discerned at all. The Anderson shelter, that pioneer device born in such rampant hope, was soon to be virtually useless for reasons quite unconnected with the German Air Force. It was all very well having an outside shelter, but not much point to it if no provision were made to render it watertight. Within a few weeks of the start of the war, half the Anderson shelters in the country were under several inches of rainwater. Within a year most of them had been abandoned to the local wildlife, and their owners obliged to find other ways of protecting themselves. In January 1941, halfway through the second soggy winter of the war, Wembley Council finally decided to scrap all the Anderson shelters on their Manor Park estate and provide indoor alternatives complete with bunks, here enjoyed by four damp young residents.

Meanwhile, 'Somewhere in the Home Counties', five hundred small girls, newly evacuated from London, enjoy the cramped bathing arrangements in what is virtually a custom-built village, containing its own farm, dairy, bakery, power plant, laundry and clothing depot. In Dover, bombed so regularly that it became known as 'Hellfire Corner', the successive waves of evacuation have by no means stripped the town of its juvenile population, which lolls around the street corner sucking sweets, manipulating toy ducks, motor cars and home-made swords, squatting on sandbags, reading comics and watching the war go by.

It has been said more than once by incredulous foreigners that the British treat their children like dogs and their dogs like children, a view substantiated by the care with which wartime members of the Canine Defence League have designed a gas box into which pooches may be popped in the event of a gas attack by some rival breed. The flap at the top of the box is covered by a cloth soaked in water, and the flaps at the side open if required, especially by the dog. As for the implications of the photograph of the mother with child perambulating through a gas-masked universe, these remain inscrutable. Was this an unpublicised incident in which the enemy did after all resort to gas as an offensive weapon? Has a quantity of the tear gas advertised on the notice board accidentally escaped from a nearby cinema where they are showing a James Cagney gangster feature? It seems more probable that some sort of war game is in progress with all citizens required to join in. By 1941 it seemed apparent to almost everyone that poison gas attacks had already drifted into the realm of the highly improbable. The habit of carrying a gas mask with you wherever you went was already beginning to crumble, and the general view accorded less with the Civil Defence zealots than with Groucho Marx, who, in a pre-war film constantly revived throughout the war, having been told that General Smith has reported a gas attack, responded with 'Tell him to take two bicarbonate of soda'.

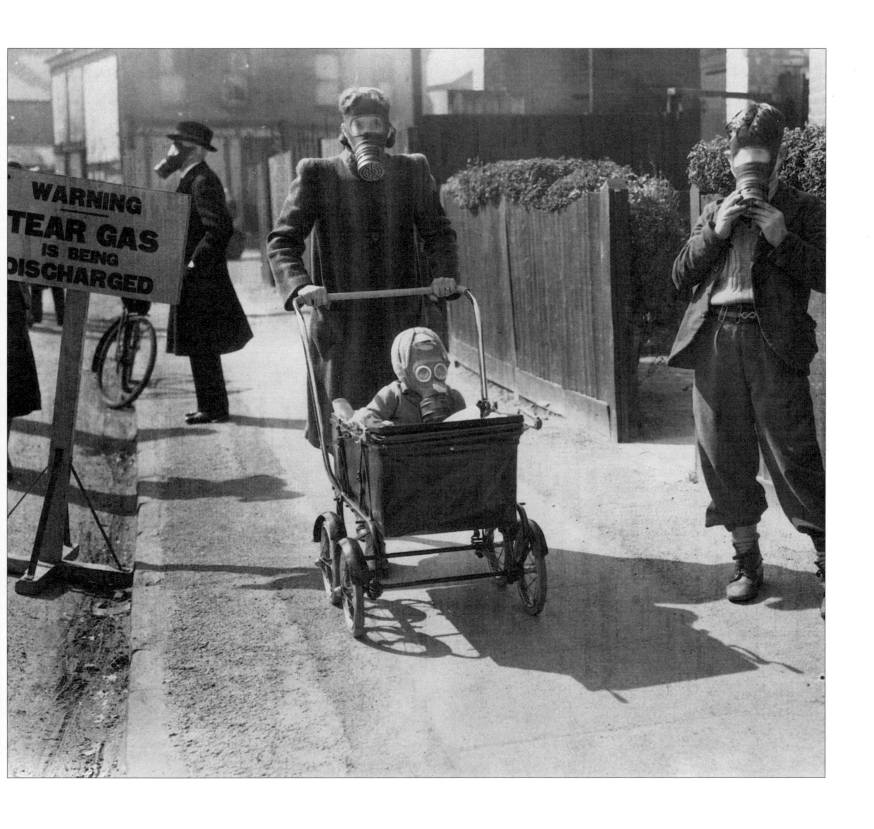

Nevertheless, the official view was that the population should be prepared for the worst. But not all of the time. At one point the Gloucestershire police were instructed to wear their respirators while on duty only on certain days in the week. This bizarre command was passed down in April 1941, with the additional order that a rhetorical question, which does seem to be a shade ambiguous, be on display on the respirator bag. The picture seems to cause more confusion than it resolves. The policeman's face remains unseen, so we cannot tell whether he is unmasked or sporting a mask cleverly disguised as a policeman's helmet. As for the pedestrian, that might just possibly be a mask on his face, or perhaps no more than an expression of incredulity.

There is no doubt, however, when it comes to the ladies on the streets of Esher in Surrey, April 1941. In fact it is April 5th, and that warden-nurse is clearly attempting to hide the baby in a place where the Inland Revenue will never find him. And while she minds the baby, mother attends to her son, and foolishly attempts a conversation while doing so. As the people of Britain quickly discovered, conversing in a gas mask was, as Beachcomber might have said, like playing a trombone under water, not only impossible but offensive. Gas-masked *tete-a-tetes* invariably ended in a succession of vaguely Rabelaisian glugging noises and the steaming up of the eyepiece, often causing nasty collisions. Such exercises were known as gas exercises by the Civil Defence authorities and by other, unmentionable, names by the population at large.

Occasionally the local Civil Defence organisations added a frisson of the unexpected to the pleasures of gas-mask practice. In this scene of a June morning in the streets of Kingston in Surrey, a mother runs to do her duty by her baby as the pair of them are caught up in what was defined, with a nice touch of euphemism, as a 'surprise gas test'. But all gas tests held surprises of assorted kinds, although the only practical contribution they could conceivably have made to the war effort was to provide the government's propaganda arm with photographic proof that the people of Britain remained on each other's toes. In that same month of June 1941, children at the L.C.C. school in Conway Street in Marylebone are seen receiving a lesson in how to apply their gas masks. The solicitude which the government was showing for the welfare of these children is deeply touching, but it is passing strange that officialdom, which throughout the twentieth century had been pleased to leave the working-class population of its capital city to survive as best it could, should suddenly have shown such concern for the children of the poor. Conway Street lay in the tangled web of slum streets between the Edgware Road and Baker Street; its festering domestic architecture, its appalling sanitary arrangements, its depressed quality of life, were a disgrace to any caring society – except that Britain was not a caring society. It was the parents of these children who, four years later, were to express grateful thanks to Winston Churchill for leading them to victory, and then to elect the country's first ever Labour administration with a working majority. But for the moment the war proceeds, and the nightly fireworks display on show free of charge creates the illusion of sunrise in a Warner Brothers musical.

# 1942

If 1942 was not quite the turning point of the war, it was certainly the first year in which the British could contemplate realistically the prospect, however distant, of eventual victory. Two events had occurred in 1941 to amend the entire course of the war. In June Hitler had unwittingly signed his own death warrant by invading the Soviet Union. And on December 7th, the Japanese warlords, by making a unilateral strike against the United States Pacific Fleet based at Pearl Harbor, did at a stroke what no British statesman had managed to do: closed the mouth of the isolationist lobby and brought the United States into the fight. Ever since the fall of France and the Low Countries, the British had been the only nation left to fight the Axis powers. A famous David Low cartoon had shown Churchill rolling up his sleeves, with the nation behind him. The caption read: 'All behind you, Winston'. And now, with the two most powerful states in the world aligned alongside the British, the future looked much more promising. As the Oxford History of England says of the folly of Pearl Harbor: 'No greater service was ever performed for the British cause. The doubts of the American people were resolved for them. They were in the war whether they would or no'.

The new feelings were well expressed by two incidents, one at the start of 1942, the other at the very end of the year. On January 1st, 1942, President Roosevelt coined a phrase to define the associated powers ranged against the Axis: The United Nations. And in December Churchill, speechifying in celebration of a spectacular victory of British arms in the Western Desert, told the nation: 'This is not the end. It is not even the beginning of the end. But it is, perhaps, the end of the beginning'. But 1942 also saw one of the most shameful episodes in British military history. The Japanese advanced down the Malay peninsula, arrived before Singapore, and received the surrender of the British garrison of 60,000 men. The surrender marked the moment when the myth of Empire lost its power among its Eastern subjects. To console the British was the promotion to command of the Eighth Army of General Bernard Law Montgomery, who made his stand at El Alemein, sixty miles from Alexandria, threw back Rommel's army, and, on October 23rd, took the offensive. Within a week Rommel was in flight and Egypt secure at last. Within a fortnight Allied forces had landed in North Africa.

On the Home Front white bread became a rarity, there was talk of coal rationing, which never happened, and, at a few by-elections, government candidates were defeated by Independents. The key words of the time were Austerity and Unity. But the ladies remained indomitable in the long struggle to ensnare the male. This young woman being disfigured in a Croydon department store hopes to create the illusion of nylons where no nylon is.

A list of the occupations which learned to accept women during the war still makes remarkable reading. One lady who rose to become an inspector on the railways was fond of recalling her first attendance at a Union branch meeting, where her gender so upset the rigid constitutional procedures that nobody knew how to address her. Eventually she found herself referred to as 'Sister'. Ladies who volunteered to fly aeroplanes faced much sterner opposition. Once an aircraft was built, someone had to fly it from the factory to the airfield. The RAF was too busy with other duties, and so a force of lady pilots proved an admirable solution. But entrenched prejudice could make things difficult. The giant intellect who edited a periodical called A*eroplane* wrote that it was ridiculous to expect women to pilot a high-speed bomber when some of them were not intelligent enough to scrub a floor. People took note that there were also some men who could not properly edit a magazine. Women became influential civil servants, perfectly able shop stewards, and were so brave about the whole business that not even the bad language, which some of them had never heard before, could deter them from the execution of their wartime duties. Perhaps there is something symbolic about the fact that the girls working on the giant wing of a Short Sunderland flying boat are on a more elevated plane than the man directing operations. There are no men in sight at all in the shot of a quartet of earnest WRNS working on the ammunition belts required to equip the light coastal craft policing home waters. Recruiting posters often tended to be romantic. The lady featured in an ARP recruiting poster looks less like a warden than a siren, while the blonde who wears a steel helmet in the Maclean's toothpaste advertisement seems set to sign a movie contract at any moment.

'Onward Christian Soldiers', solemnly intoned the patriotic choirs of both sides in the war, and with every chorus some ancient church went down in a mass of flame and rubble. The anomalies of the Church in war have diverted satirists for generations, and the fact that nations whose Established Church commands its brethren 'Thou Shalt Not Kill' should employ priests to sanctify the killing is not one which logicians have been able to make very much of. When in 1943 the British began using bomber squadrons to devastate German cities, there were fierce objections from the Archbishop of Canterbury, who was duly informed by the War Cabinet that only strategic targets were being attacked. This was true in the sense that the War Cabinet conceived anything German to be a strategic target, a view supported by most Britons. But the Archbishop was fobbed off by a diplomatic lie, for, as the Air Minister said, '...only in this way could he satisfy the inquiries of the Archbishop of Canterbury', who must have been further reassured to learn that all air stations in Britain maintained on the strength at least one Anglican chaplain. The Archbishop's compassion on the subject was little short of divine, for in 1942 he had seen the Cathedral at Canterbury badly damaged in the German cause. On the morning of June 2nd, firemen were still baptising the smouldering wreckage of the English Shrine after the previous night's raid. In the same raid the glass was blasted from the Cathedral windows.

Much starker tragedy had visited the London borough of Leytonstone four months before, when the pilot of an RAF plane, attempting to crash-land on open ground, missed his target and came down on a street, shattering a house and a concert-hall. On the morning after, the fires have been put out, but the plane crew and five civilians will never live to tell the tale.

There was more than one Albert Memorial. His effigy was raised in bronze at Holborn Circus, in white marble inside the Royal Exchange, on horseback in Wolverhampton, holding a gun at Balmoral, in Aberdeen doing nothing in particular, and so on. Less obvious memorials demanded by his widow included a published edition of his collected speeches and an account written by the Queen, with a little help from her friends, of her life with Albert. But by far the most spectacular folly of all was the Albert Memorial in Hyde Park, a grandiloquent structure which puzzles the onlooker more and more as the years advance and the memory of Albert means less and less. The memorial took eight years to complete, and includes representations of 169 great men of Albert's time, or whose reputations stood high during his marriage to Victoria. The structure consists of granite, sandstone, slate, marble and limestone. It proved almost impervious to German bombs, the only damage it sustained being the removal of Asia's breast. The memorial is so monstrous that the sculptor Epstein used to doff his hat to it every time he passed by. Victoria regarded the memorial as a holy place, and would never have permitted her people to deploy the foreground to the memorial as a site for growing peas. But by the spring of 1942 the Queen was long since gone, and peas were considered more important than the memory of a dead consort.

Everyone grew vegetables now in their allotments, even those engaged on vital war work. In the City of London, firemen at the Redcross Street station used the bomb-scarred sites themselves as the base of their operations, producing one of the neatest allotments in London.

Balancing the lurid tales of maltreated evacuees, disenchanted evacuees, bored evacuees and homesick evacuees, all of whom decamped within months or even weeks of being uprooted, and went scurrying back to the more familiar comforts of mean streets, there was the occasional romance concerning some little townie for whom the experience of evacuation meant a first glimpse of the countryside. These converts to the rustic life were sometimes said to have become so enchanted with pigs and fertilizer that they refused ever to go home again, preferring instead to reverse the trend of the previous hundred years and start their own drift from town to country. But the gesture was eccentric for all the sincerity of their love of the greenery. In 1851, the year of Prince Albert's brainchild, the Great Exhibition, Great Britain became the first society in the history of the world to have more town than country dwellers, and the few fundamentalists of the evacuation scheme who went back to someone else's roots were flying in the face of history, which is, of course, sometimes a very exhilarating thing to do. The London schoolboys who found their way to Tweenaway School, Paignton, in Devon, showed an almost indecent expertise in the art of inducing marrows to swell beyond their normal size. As a marrow is a boring thing to eat, the larger it gets the worse it becomes, yet these well-meaning lads have managed a pair weighing fifty-four and forty-five pounds respectively. As though this were not enough, the pumpkin shown standing guard over them also weighs over forty pounds. There is no information telling us what the two schoolboys weigh. Meanwhile, in Hemel Hempstead, the child farmers work in platoons, armed with rakes and shovels, like some embryonic Home Guard detachment fighting the war before the last. This group of conscripts is about to plant potatoes, suggesting that the wheelbarrow is either for show or is a trophy of some kind.

Whether or not Emperor Hirohito ever realised it, his act of starting a war with the United States had the incidental effect of destroying utterly the most dearly-cherished corpus of legend in the possession of the British. In 1942 there was still no television to corrupt the innocence of the locals, and travel to America was still so exotic an affair that to the mass of the population it seemed completely beyond the bounds of reality. New York might have been on the far side of the moon for all the practical application it had to life in Britain. And yet the British believed that they knew America very well, even intimately. They knew all about American politics because James Stewart had educated them. They knew all about American jurisprudence because Gene Lockhart had said 'Objection overruled' a thousand times. They knew that all American waitresses were beautiful because Jean Harlow and Carole Lombard were the living proof. They knew that Raymond Walburn was a chortling, Deep South senator so crooked that he could hide at will behind a spiral staircase, that Patsy Kelly laboured as a cook in the kitchens of a rich house, that Leonid Kinsky was a Russian émigré determined never to go to work. They believed you had only to go to Forty-Second Street to find Ruby Keeler and Alice Faye shouting at James Cagney and Dick Powell, and that somewhere, on some black-and-white terrace bathed in moonlight, Fred was dancing with Ginger. The British attended their local cinema in the same spirit that their forefathers had once attended church, in the hope of being received into a state of grace, or at any rate Grace Moore. No American then or since has understood the proposition that the British, having swallowed the Hollywood version of history hook, line and sinker, were astonished, dismayed and angry when they were confronted by real Americans and noted the differences.

Once America entered the war, Roosevelt committed himself to the Churchillian theory that the key to victory was the destruction of Germany. Which meant war in Europe. Which meant the transportation of millions of American soldiers to Britain. At first the euphoria was hysterical. Each GI was Tyrone Power or Andy Devine, only for real. This mood of idiotic receptivity lasted between four and five minutes, after which 'Got any gum, chum', was amended to 'Overpaid, oversexed and over here'. No American soldier could possibly live up to the image vouchsafed to the British by the likes of Gable and Cooper, not even the GIs who, in October 1942, threw a party for the kids of the East End, giving away their own sweet ration to the youngsters. But the friendly soldier has committed the arch crime of not being Tyrone Power. His cause is lost. The British stolidly saw it through, even persisting in their amazing gift for ugly headwear. The Putney Girl Guides, helmeted like all girl guides, dig doggedly to victory on their allotment belonging to the local hospital. When the produce is ready for picking the guides will carry it into the kitchens, help cook it, and then help serve it to the patients. Not even Irene Dunne could do more.

More than any previous war in history, 1939-45 was a struggle between rival mechanics. The sophistication of mechanized warfare would have amazed the men who marched to South Africa with General Buller, or who marched to perdition with General Haig. Some idea of how far the construction of mobile weaponry had come by the autumn of 1942 is conveyed by the photograph of Mrs Lilian Evans, propelling her machine in the general direction of the front – the front of the machine, that is. Mrs Evans is one of the intrepid outriders of the Women's Voluntary Service, and her ingenuity knows no bounds. Her mobile storeroom is a converted ice cream cart, and her uniform has been specially designed along seductive lines in order to distract any amorous enemies from the true nature of her work. It is October 14th, and in just twenty-six days from now Mrs Evans will take office as Mayor of Dagenham, although her Aldermanic duties will never entirely remove her from the saddle.

The Women's Voluntary Service has outposts all over the four kingdoms, performing useful work in tending the old, the sick, the very young; delivering food to those who are in need of it and performing the thousand-and-one duties which can never be covered by Acts of Parliament. The Southgate branch is busy making jam in their improvised factory in the village hall. The jam, when bottled, will be sent to the local Food Office, from where it will be sent to another Food Office and then another, and so on until it is time to make more jam. Those bottles that the jam is going into, they may look like common or garden jam jars. But this is war, and war things are rarely common and never ever garden. Those innocent-looking jars are in reality nothing less than 'special Ministry of Food containers'.

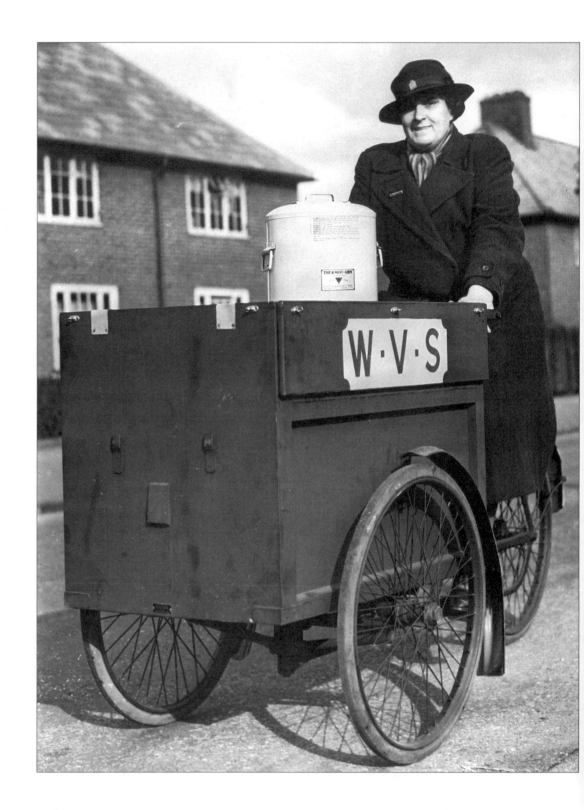

When war broke out the government was over-generous in its assessment of how much food would be required to feed everyone. The eventual figures showed that Britain could get along comfortably enough on a million or two tons less of nutrition than the politicians had thought. One of several factors which helped keep the British healthy, if not gorged, was the farming of millions of acres of land which had been lying fallow. But though the land was there for the growing, where was the labour? The Women's Land Army marched on to the arable land of the country and soon transformed the labour problem. Their usefulness was unarguable, their efficiency priceless. But even so, they were constantly under pressure to prove themselves, which is what is happening in the central photograph. One day in July, 1942, the ladies of the Land Army in West Suffolk give a demonstration of their prowess in all forms of land work. Here they trundle happily away, forking silage into a silo.

To the left the line advances across the Sussex countryside as the local contingent gathers in the harvest, looking less like farmers than the ladies of one of C.B. Cochran's chorus performing a dance with a vaguely agricultural theme. On the right another troupe struggles to mastery over a mountain of hay.

The barrage balloon looked like a joke. Flopping around at its moorings like some stage elephant, or sitting up there in the sky, vaguely reminiscent of Walt Disney's Dumbo in the moment when he achieved flight, the barrage balloon served a vital tactical function after all. One of the deadliest forms of aerial attack was the dive-bombing of large cities. The *Luftwaffe* had had some practice at this noble art during the Spanish Civil War. But the presence of rows of barrage balloons made dive-bombing a hopeless impracticability. Any attacking aircraft attempting to fly low would find itself enmeshed in the folds or cables of this odd contraption and would crash to its doom. The effect which the balloons had was usually unnoticed because it was a negative effect. It prevented something happening. But it was an ingenious if simple way of saving civilian lives. It required nobody to be on board and only a small ground staff to manipulate its whimsical choreography. There was one moored at the City Temple, manned by girls from the WAAF, who are seen here bringing the tame monster to earth.

The armies which decamped for foreign fields between 1939 and 1945 comprised a genuine citizens' army. In this photograph of serving men waiting to board ship for some remote theatre of war, poet jostles peasant, bank clerk finds himself cheek by jowl with barrowboy, insurance salesman squats next to professional footballer. All the disparate groups of Civvy Street came together in common cause. How many of the men in this group lived to exercise their right to vote? How many were left on the beaches at Dunkirk, at Dieppe, at Anzio and in Normandy? Who knows? But each man in the photograph retains that naive faith in his own immortality and smiles, either because so far the war has been a bit of a pleasant change, or because it is a relief to get away from the wife.

One of the golden rules of London life is never to go looking for a taxi on Yom Kippur. In 1942 the rule was extended to embrace also October 6th. On that day hundreds of London cabbies, all members of the same Home Guard Unit, including officers and NCOs, forsook their passengers and took part in a large-scale war game involving a German force which had established a bridgehead at, of all place, Southend. The job of the cabbies was to stop the German advance through Epping Forest. In this noble enterprise they were assisted by hundreds of lorries from the London District Transport Column, whose allotted task was to rush ammunition and supplies up to the forest, as well as to deliver reinforcements. This was the first exercise involving an imaginary invasion to include the taxi drivers, who did their work with some efficiency, reaching their locations, displaying their Great War medal ribbons, patching up holes in the roofs of their vehicles with bits of foliage, and generally having a much better time of it than the Germans would have, had they been foolish enough to land at Southend. The man lying down in front of a taxi with the apparent intention of asking the driver to take him somewhere beyond the seven mile limit, is in effect pretending to be a German who is still looking for Southend. War, to judge from the expressions on the faces of the battling cabbies, is a comical business.

One of the vital links in Britain's air defences was the Observer Corps, an army of enthusiasts whose job it was to monitor the coastal skies twenty-four hours a day, identifying any enemy aircraft approaching. The men of the corps would then transmit their information to the nearest airfields, giving them due warning of the type of aircraft approaching, how many planes there were, and its likely destination. It was particularly important for the defending squadrons to know what kind of opposition was on its way, and the men of the Observer Corps were trained to glance up at a plane and assess all its vital statistics. This art of instantaneous recognition was acquired only after long hours of homework, studying charts on which were printed the silhouettes of all known enemy aeroplanes. As each fighter and bomber had a distinctive outline quite unlike any other, the observer was able to match what he saw above him with the silhouettes on the identification chart. Their skill was sometimes acquired in tender youth, for the Air Training Corps, an organisation consisting of pre-conscription boys, distributed the identification charts to all its squadrons. Very often a boy entering the RAF after a spell in the ATC was perfectly capable of taking his place as a fully qualified observer. Usually, however, he was made an apprentice cook or a carpenter. The Observer Corps performed its duties in a quaint way, simply by stargazing, but there was never any question of the essential nature of its performance. In the photograph, an observer at a lonely hilltop outpost scans the cloudscapes while his companion stands guard.

Often during the war there were sentimental echoes of a way of peaceful life which would never return. In April 1942 the Cunliffe-Owen stud farm at Bray, near Maidenhead, flung out a *cri de coeur* which did not go unanswered. The paddocks, in which famous racehorses had once frisked, were now converted to agriculture, and the owners found themselves obliged to appeal for help from the War Office when the harvest was ready to be gathered. Help was duly sent, and the soldiers doing their stuff may or may not have been aware that they are working on land hallowed in the minds of every horseplayer in the land. It was on this grass that the great Derby winner Felsted had once cut his capers. The work being performed by the soldiers is peaceful enough, and it was often clear that for aspects of bellicosity it was wise to turn to the amateurs, the part-timers and the volunteers. That London Transport should ever have possessed a force of trained Commandos may have come as a surprise to some, but these members of the troop certainly have all the aspects of deadly ferocity required for the job. They all carry knives as well as rifles and bayonets, and all are trained in unarmed combat. Had there ever been an invasion, they would certainly have been among the defenders. Nor was the training wasted. Once these bus drivers and conductors returned to civilian life, they found their military training of great practical use during the rush hour.

# 1943

For the British people the new year dawned in promise. Montgomery had won his place in history at Alamein, and the world looked on in awed disbelief as the German army bled to death in the ruined streets of Stalingrad. A cosmic bookmaker, asked to quote odds in the race for victory, would have granted the British even money at the very least. This was the year of meetings of the war leaders at Casablanca and Teheran and of the sudden familiarity of that ominous piece of rhetoric, 'Unconditional Surrender'. It was the year when the government became so confident that the danger of invasion had receded out of sight that it lifted the ban on the ringing of church bells. In the time of the threat of an invasion, the ringing of church bells was to be the signal that German forces had landed. As from April 19th, once again the clangour in the belfrey contained merely religious overtones. 1943 was the year in which widespread public support was voiced for the Beveridge Report, which promised substantial advances towards the social fair shares which the mass of people dreamed about; a year in which industrial unrest in the mining industry suggested that the truce induced by the war might be drawing to a close; a year in which Independent candidates won by-elections, and the first of the Axis powers sued for peace. At the beginning of July the Allied armies invaded Italy; before the end of the month Mussolini had been deposed. In September Italy surrendered. One down, two to go, said the comedians. But before the Allies could occupy Italy, the German army had moved in, prepared for one of the bloodiest last-ditch battles of the war. And if the year threw up one phrase of historical significance, it was 'Second Front Now', meaning an Allied invasion of Europe to relieve the Soviet armies and to crush the Germans by waging a war on two fronts.

And yet at a deeper level 1943 was a tragic year, in which Britain took its last sobbing breath as a world power; a year in which for the first time it was sustained by American money, power, industry, shipping, food, tools; a year in which the leadership of the Allies became a duet between Roosevelt and Stalin, with Churchill doing what he could to uphold the British cause. It was the year in which the U-Boat menace was largely overcome, again largely through American sea and air power. And it was the year in which two features of post-war life first reared their unlovely heads. The tax collecting system known as 'Pay As You Earn' or PAYE, first became operative, and during the year there arose the ministry of Town and Country Planning.

But the population at large merely sensed it was winning at last. The young lady in the 'Utility' costume, the girl sitting on the ground enjoying a cup of tea and the young lady perched on her upturned suitcase, are all queueing at Waterloo, waiting for hours on the last morning of July, hoping to reach the coat and sniff a few lungfuls of sea air.

But even if your train did arrive, and even if you managed to get on it, and even if it arrived at its advertised destination – by the sea – there was still no guarantee that your expectations of a dip would be fulfilled. Along the eastern flank of England, which looked across the water to Europe and the possible threat of invasion, the sea coasts had been disfigured in the name of wartime precautions. Observation posts usurped the ice cream huts, and bomb-proof concrete bunkers replaced the deck chair repositories. And squirming like a poisonous snake along the coastline was the barbed wire, proclaiming the glum truth that beachcombers were not here to enjoy themselves but to repel boarders. Much of this detritus of defence could still be seen long years into the peace, symbols of defiance allowed to degenerate into eyesores instead of being removed as speedily as they had been erected. The pillboxes became silted up, and the observation posts no more than a port of call for the wheeling gulls, and a godsend perhaps for small boys in search of bit of harmless war-game tomfoolery.

On August 1st, a day after the patient ladies took up their positions in the queue at Waterloo Station, two young mothers accompanied by two young daughters set off from West Kensington to reach the east coast, only to find when they arrived there that they might just as well have stayed home for all the pleasures of the shingle they were to be allowed to enjoy. They had been unfortunate enough to choose a spot where the military had barred entry onto the beach, and declared the sea a danger zone. The younger of the two girls, all dressed for immersion, is so saddened by the deprivation that she sheds a few tears for the injustices of this life, and no doubt vows that when she grows up she will organise things a bit more efficiently than these pathetic adults.

In the 1930s in Britain there was a popular song called *Why Did She Fall for the Leader of the Band?*. In those days as a general rule dance-band leaders were either musical poseurs or bow-tied popinjays. The profile of this extraordinary musical type was high because of his insistence on standing in front of the orchestra waving a baton. For any leader of any strict-tempo orchestra to resort to a baton is a dismal admission of failure. To wave it at the audience instead of at the musicians, as most leaders tended to do, amounted to charlatanism of truly wondrous proportions. But the kudos of leadership, added to the fact that nobody else's name was on the posters, gave fame to the band leader. With the war came a variation on this theme. Most units included in their muster enough musicians to form a station dance band, usually with names like the Modernaires, or the Quavertones, or the Swingettes. They would play for their fellows at Saturday night hops and play a few chords with the required gravitas at church services. Often the serviceman-musician was regarded as a shrewd operator who had used his musical expertise to acquire a soft option. The 605 Squadron band was unusual in that its title incorporated at least half the leader's name.

The Cliff responsible for this conspiracy of crotchets was Cliff Hughes, seen here sitting at the piano with the curiously detached composure of the born band leader. The phenomenon of the pianist-leader presented serious problems in the propagation of the personality cult. If a man was seated at the keyboard, how could he also stand up and wave his arms about? Some famous leaders solved the problem by hiring another pianist. Others gave up playing the piano altogether, which was usually a blessing to others. But sometimes the pianist of a servicemen's band ascended to the leadership because of his musical knowledge. While the members of the orchestra are capable of playing only one note at a time, if that, the pianist can play several simultaneously, which gives him a much better chance of grasping the principles of harmony, which means in turn that he can act as orchestrator as well as pianist.

Among the songs being churned out by bands like the Crotchets would have been *Be Careful, It's My Heart, Dearly Beloved, He's My Guy, I Don't Want to Walk Without You, Moonlight Becomes You, My Devotion, Skylark, That Old Black Magic* and the interminable *White Christmas*. There would have been also some quasi-patriotic songs like *He Wears a Pair of Silver Wings, Praise the Lord and Pass the Ammunition, Silver Wings in the Moonlight*, and of course *We'll Meet Again*. And the leader, if he had the right stuff in him, might even have made a stab at *The Warsaw Concerto*. The entertainment provided by this type of band was perfectly innocent, its income negligible, its duties sometimes onerous. Yet there were those who wished that they too had learned an instrument well enough to get into a service orchestra and sidestep the flak. Cliff Hughes was killed on Christmas Eve, 1943, flying over Berlin.

Sometimes, in an effort to bring home to the civilian population the sheer magnitude of the act of faith required to take a heavy bomber into the air, the propaganda manipulators would wheel in a famous specimen to the centre of a large town, where it would perch like some great bird, inducing such gasps of wonder from the onlookers that they would be an easy touch when it came to contributing to National Savings. Throughout the war the general population was entreated to 'Save for Victory', and it always responded in the required spirit. National Savings had first been introduced in 1917 by a politician called Andrew Bonar Law, the possessor of a personality so scintillating that he is remembered as 'The Unknown Prime Minister'. This unkind label was stuck on him by a professional rival called Mr Asquith, to which posterity can only respond by murmuring to itself, 'look who's talking'. 'In the Second World War', says Professor Alan Taylor, 'a poster appealing for National Savings was as characteristic as Kitchener's glowering face had been in the first war'. The savings campaigns were usually successful, but the view of later historians, that the reason was partly the lack of things on which to spend money, is not altogether borne out by the facts. One of the most desirable commodities in war was food, and as there were restaurants and cafes open, there was always something enjoyable available if you wished to spend a little surplus cash. In these photographs, the star is *H for Harry*, a much publicised Sterling bomber which had created a record of sixty-seven operational flights. It was with a nice sense of punctilio that *H for Harry* was located outside the cathedral more famous than any other in Britain as the symbol of a religion which recommends the turning of the other cheek.

The saturation bombing of Britain's major cities in 1940-41 had one effect on morale which would have surprised the advocates of such tactics. Those millions who survived the terrible ordeal to which they were subjected by the *Luftwaffe*, acquired, almost without realising it, a resilience under fire amounting almost to truculence. It was rooted in the most logical of propositions. If, having been subjected to the threat of being blown limb from limb every night for months, they were still here, then why lose sleep over the occasional air raid? Not until the summer of 1944 and the appearance of a fresh variation in the art of destroying the innocent did the people in the large towns show much concern. For some the habits of survival acquired during the Blitz were so ingrained as to have become a ritual; for the rest of the war these people continued to retire nightly to their local underground station, or at any rate to run to the nearest shelter the moment the banshee wail of the warning sirens quickened the pulse. But in London by 1943 the overwhelming majority of the population slept in their own beds, preferring the snugness of home rather than chance the possibility of catching a cold running around the streets in the small hours.

On the night of October 17th, 1943, London suffered an air raid which was reported in the next morning's newspapers. People read that 'a few enemy planes' were seen, and that 'a few bombs were dropped on the London area', but that there had been 'only slight damage'. But slight in comparison to what? In the context of the Blitz this belittling of the raid was logical enough, but it was also true that for those who suffered on the night of October 17th the ferocity of the advent of the bombs was as terrible as anything that had happened before. On that night, even though there were only a few planes dropping a few bombs, people still died, were still buried alive, were still burnt to death, were still blown through their own walls. Or, if they were blessedly fortunate, they suffered nothing more than the experience of seeing their homes blown to smithereens, their possession damaged beyond repair, their lives breached once and for all. One of the most graphic photographs of the war was taken in the aftermath of the raid of October 17th. It features Sergeant Robson of the Metropolitan Police, whose duties that night and the following morning included the search to find life among the debris. A woman has been identified, still alive but buried under the rubble. The Sergeant has been trying to rescue her. At last, exhausted by his despairing efforts, he takes a breather, his jacket encrusted with the dust of the raid, his helmet gripped by his hand resting on his knee. What is he thinking of as he sits there trying to muster the energy to continue the search? Whatever it is, it can have little to do with his mood when, in the days of peace, he enlisted with the force. While he sits there contemplating the joys of civilised life in the twentieth century, his colleagues in the ARP continue to poke around in the wreckage, in the forlorn hope of discovering a live person.

Early morning in a London street. The all-clear siren signals your release from the local shelter, where you have been dozing fitfully in your clothes, vaguely aware that your dreams are being punctuated by crumps and crashes. You emerge from your shelter not knowing what to expect but sensing the worst. But it is nothing. Your home has been knocked down, that is all. The roof balances itself against the ground floor wreckage at an angle of forty-five degrees. The door frames are scattered around the ground. So you do what you can to retrieve any bits and pieces which the enemy has been negligent enough to overlook. There is the kitchen table and a few chairs. A cake-baking tin, a scrubbing brush, a suitcase tied with string, a wardrobe with its mirror miraculously uncracked. And, standing there comically impervious to the nightmare, a dressmaker's headless dummy awaiting further instructions and pins. Not much to build a new life with, but at least you have that life, which is more than can be said for the twelve dead children found in the wreckage of an L.C.C. school on a January morning. The bombers skimmed the rooftops in a surprise daylight attack, scoring a memorable victory over a few small boys in short pants and a few of their sweethearts in cotton dresses. A week before this neat exercise in barbarism, Mrs Wingrave, a London housewife who has spent the night in the shelter with her family, pauses in her researches to contemplate the rearrangements which have been made to her front window. At least when she starts life again she will still have that pastoral scene to put on the kitchen wall.

As the United States army and air force poured into Britain, authorities on both sides strove anxiously to maintain mutual goodwill. A feeling of resentment against American servicemen was sometimes apparent. They were better paid than British soldiers, better dressed, and carried with them, all unconsciously, that vicarious glamour of the movies which reduced so many amorous young ladies to the last extremity of passion. None of this was the fault of the visitors, who did, however, sometimes seem to be unaware that the war had been going on for a little while before they had so much as seen a uniform. The lurid tales of inter-allied pub brawls and rowdiness were balanced by carefully photographed scenes of philosophic intent, incidents of impeccable do-goodery which seem devalued in some odd way by the very presence of the engines of propaganda. At an American Army Air Force station somewhere in England, two hundred English children orphaned by the Blitz are invited to squadron headquarters to be entertained by the serving men. Each American was designated father for the day to five of the orphans, most of whom seem to be members of a military outfit themselves.

The American servicemen who were garrisoned in Britain were the first from their country to see, and occasionally to experience, the traumas of air raids. But by 1943 the raids had dropped off, leaving only the old blitzed areas to be enjoyed as local sights. Seven GIs, dwarfed by the shadow of St Paul's, strike a suitably reverent pose in the face of strewn wreckage. It must have made a great snapshot to send to the folks back home.

'Britain's Finest Hour', they called it, for the very good reason that it was genuinely a people's war, in the sense that virtually everyone capable of contributing something did so. Among the saddest duties to be performed was the very necessary sustaining of the spirits of Allied prisoners of war. Among the more prominent groups to be responsible for this duty was the Navy, Army and Air Force Institution, abbreviated to the NAAFI, an organisation which did everything from sending small luxuries to overseas soldiers, sailors and airmen, to administering garrison canteens in which there was usually an upright piano, usually out of tune, always beer-stained, and a selection of food slightly different from military rations, and available at absurdly cheap prices. The NAAFI tended to be derided affectionately by the British, who liked to compare the antiquity of its sandwiches with those of the London and North Eastern Railway, the texture of its rock-cakes with rock, and the potency of its tea with a tot of whisky. In later years, the derogatory term 'naff' became popular among the British middle classes; this may have been an unconscious reference to the friendly opprobrium in which the NAAFI was held. The girls in white pinafores are spending an October morning packing boxes of cigarettes to be sent to British prisoners of war in time for Christmas. The girls of Parkfield Cedars School, meanwhile, have given up two weeks of the holidays to help out at a Royal Ordnance factory. These supplies are required in a hurry by the Allied forces in Sicily.

Among the more spectacular idiocies connected with the direction of labour in wartime Britain, none drew more raspberries, nor so richly deserved them, than the scheme implemented by the indecently spherical Minister of Labour, Ernest Bevin, who decreed that when teenagers reached the age of eighteen and became liable for conscription, they be given the opportunity, as it was laughingly called, to become coal miners. The drawbacks to spending hours at a time deep underground breathing in coal dust were all too obvious, but there were the consolatory factors of an absence of army discipline and regulations, and the chance to practice a little traditional absenteeism once the embryonic miner became conversant with the system. The young transport worker at the head of this queue at Southwark Labour Exchange patiently waits to hand over his identity card, while the clerk at the desk, disguised as Clement Attlee, tries a new trick with his fountain pen: writing out rubbish in quintuplicate. Candidates were invited to express a preference for Navy, Air Force or coal mines, there already being more soldiers in the army than the government knew what to do with. Once the conscript had expressed his preference, every care was taken to ensure that he was put somewhere else. The young lads on their first visit to the pit face have been given steel helmets in case the roof caves in, and lamps in case the power fails. By such means did the authorities imbue their apprentices with confidence in their new working conditions.

This cherubic little lady is gaining useful preparation for life's hard knocks by being invited to help drop a large bomb on an enemy city and very likely eliminate a lot of little girls just as strategically important as she evidently is. The bombcase is in Trafalgar Square, and the gimmick is for the general public to buy stamps and stick them on the bombcase. At the end of the week, the Post Office having made a tidy profit, the case will be removed, filled with high explosive, and dropped as a 500lb packet on the enemy. This highly civilised way of running the nation's propaganda machine seems to meet with unqualified approval from the capped boy on the left of the picture, whose exposure to the unorthodoxies of wartime diet have apparently caused his feet to grow at altogether the wrong pace. The indiscriminate bombing of Germany proved to be one of the war's great miscalculations. A Mr Harris, commander of the British bombing squadrons, was convinced that by bombing German cities the war could be won without any further fighting. In the event, the campaign was at least as damaging to British prospects as it was to those of the enemy. German night raiders took a heavy toll of the bombers, indeed losses became heavy enough to be prohibitive. Harris still insisted that bombing and bombing and bombing could bring the war to an end. At last he was deprived of his command and his bombers put under the control of General Eisenhower, who never seemed to know what to do with them.

By the end of 1943 the American presence in Britain was so overwhelming that it had become part of everyday experience. Scattered all down the east coast were American Air Force bases, from which the bombers were flying out constantly on raids over Germany. Army garrisons trained soldiers in the new arts of invasion, as talk of the Second Front rose to a crescendo of expectancy. Social exchanges between the garrisons and the locals were taken for granted. Girls from obscure villages suddenly found themselves dancing in the arms of New Yorkers who introduced them to the luxury of T-bone steaks and nylons. Very often, however, it was the locals who turned out to be sophisticates and the visitors, farm boys from the Midwestern states, the neophytes. Among the unofficial duties performed by the Americans were assorted charitable works to counterbalance any talk of asperity in the saloon bar or at the dance hall. Three American officers propagandize for the American way of life by feeding Cokes and Planter's Cocktail Peanuts to the junior population of an English village. Christmas is coming, and the children sensibly attempt to fit the seven fat years into a single afternoon. The fare at the NAAFI is much more predictable, even traditional. A uniformed Amazon smiles at the very thought of being asked to eat a slice of NAAFI cake, and her male counterparts react in the same way to the sight of Christmas mince pies distributed free of charge. When not eaten, these pies might make useful small arms in the event of a belated invasion attempt.

And we, as if you hadn't already guessed, are the Boys of the Old Brigade, veterans of the first war to end wars, participating in the second without the faintest consciousness of the irony of it all. Mr A. Davis and his colleague Mr Major are vigilance personified as they show the official photographer how the Coastguard Patrol operates. Surveillance of British shores round the clock, that is the modest function of the patrol, ever on the *qui vive* for unidentified approaching planes, fragments of wreckage on the sea's surface, floating mines, even the sudden perforation of the face of the waters by a periscope. The patrol performs especially vital work in spotting ships in distress, and the exact location of RAF pilots who have baled out into the sea. Mr Davis is taking a bearing on his specially designed dinner plate, while Mr Major, who served in the famous Dover Patrol in the Great War, looks for Mr Davis.

In Paddington, with three days left to Christmas, fifty United States soldiers are busy dispensing gifts to four hundred local schoolchildren. On a stage draped with the flags of the Allies are two beakers, which suggests that tea has already been served. The film show is yet to come. The man in the false whiskers is probably a CIA agent with a finger in every mince pie. Do these happy celebrants give a thought to the war? Hopefully not for the moment. Death was never very far away, as the residents of Goodwood in Sussex were reminded in the last days of the year, when a German bomber came plummetting to earth on the South Downs, black smoke trailing from its tail like a funereal plume.

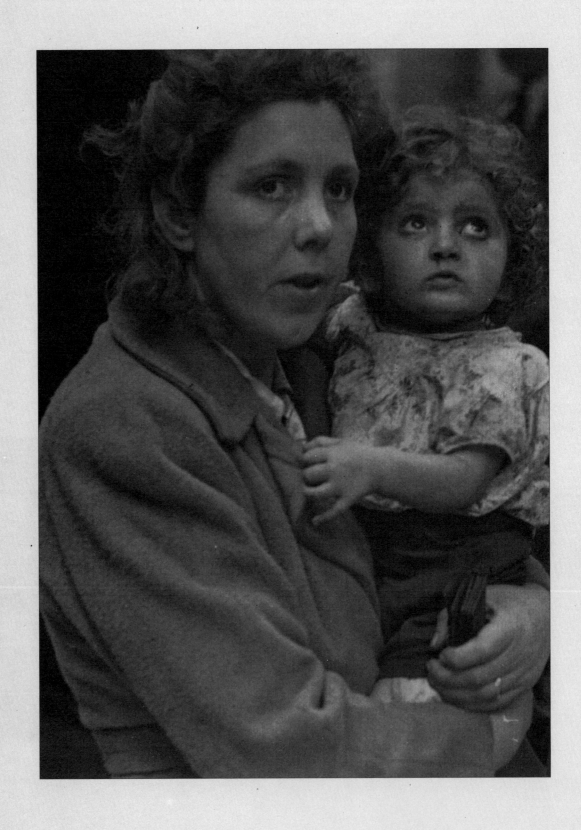

# 1944

In 1944, for the first time since the declaration of war, there were signs of weariness among the British. Considering the terrifying pressures to which they had been subjected without even a moment's respite for the past three years, it was something of a miracle that they were able to fight on with such resolution and energy. But now the senior partners in the Grand Alliance were the United States and the Soviet Union, and had it not been for the internationally-recognised magnetism of Churchill, the British role might have shrunk still further. It occurred to nobody at the time that, in assuming an equal role with its two allies, Britain was a small country aspiring to parity with two continents. History will not fail to record, however, that had it not been for British efforts till now, there would have been no Allied cause left for America and Russia to espouse. The British alone had held the Axis forces long enough for the other allies to enter the fray, in which sense if Britain could not claim to have won the war single-handed, she could certainly claim to have preserved the cause when nobody else was prepared to help.

One of the symptoms of war-weariness was the incidence of industrial unrest, which manifested itself in an increased number of strikes. The reasons for this unrest are revealing. In 1944 there grew an impatience with the conditions of war, a hunger for the coming peace, and a determination among the population at large that this time there would be no avoiding the issues. Lloyd George's hollow joke following the Great War, of a land fit for heroes to live in, must this time be secured. The miners in particular began to demand nationalization. In the words of A.J.P. Taylor: 'The British people had risen, without fuss, to unparalleled heights of sacrifice and resolution. They deserved a reward'. One installment of this reward seemed to be the 1944 Education Act, which raised the school leaving age to 15, and made grammar and technical school education free. Its more reactionary effect was to ordain for the first time that religious education in schools be compulsory.

For the immediate future, the British were to remember above all two developments in the war, one foreign, one domestic. The domestic, if the bombing of the defenceless can so be described, concerned the last German throw in the air war: pilotless rocket planes directed at Britain with enough fuel to reach inland. The engine would then cut out and the warhead plummet down at random. But the V1s, or doodle-bugs as the British derisorily referred to them, came too late. On June 6th the Allies at last landed on the European mainland in one of the most brilliantly conceived and very nearly faultlessly executed offensives in the history of modern warfare. Once again most of the credit belonged to the British, who, running against their own past military history, planned everything with imagination, creativity and skill. The final act of the war had started at last.

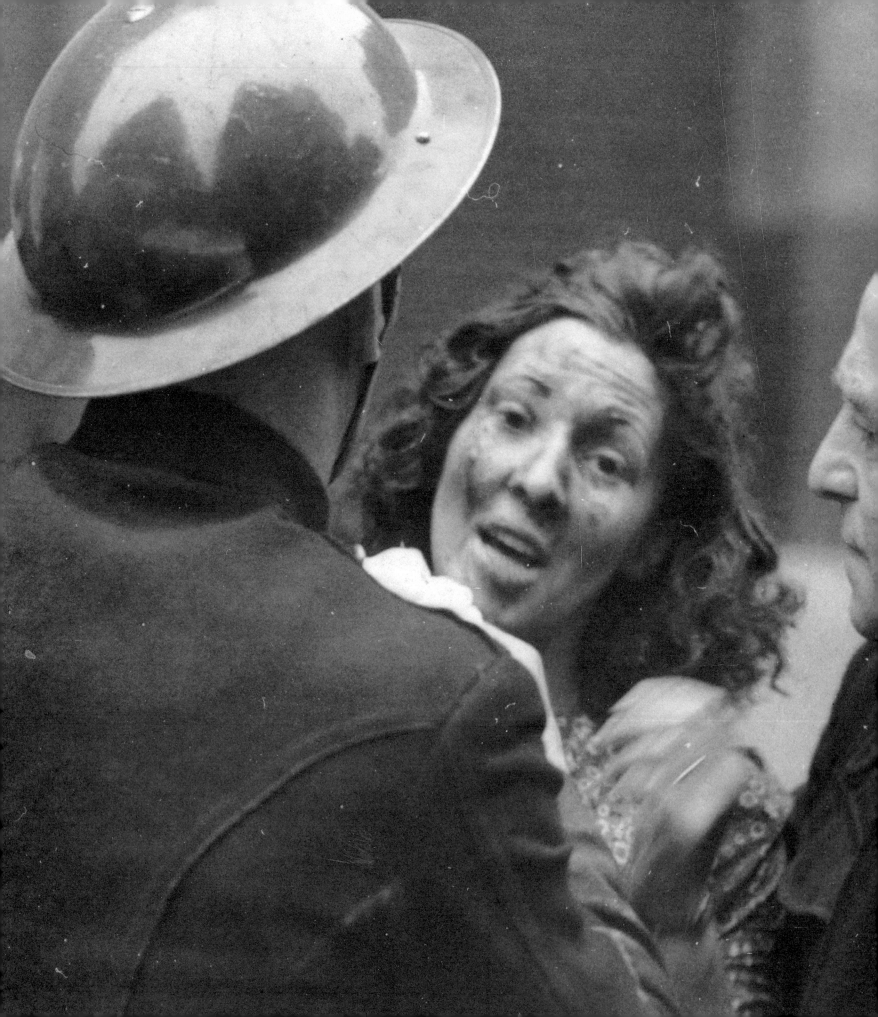

When the doodle-bugs came crashing down on London streets in broad daylight in the high summer of 1944, exploding on hospitals and schools, on shops and factories, the carnage was horrifying. There was no known defence against the pilotless planes unless a lucky interception or a random shot from an anti-aircraft gun happened to destroy them in flight. Sometimes there was not even time to sound the warning siren, so swift was their advent. The population of the south of England, and London in particular, took a deep breath and prepared to face it out once again. To most people the Blitz now seemed remote enough to back the assumption that death from the air was no longer a serious threat. Now it was to begin all over again and in a more frightening form. The outside world looked on in awe as the greatest city in the world went about its business, contemptuous of its enemy, grief-stricken, blood-spattered but resolute. Between 1939 and 1945 the British weathered so many crises, mouthed such defiance in the face of superior forces, supped with death so often without a tremor, that it is difficult to know what really was 'Their Finest Hour'. Churchill had used the phrase with reference to the Blitz, but it was the same brand of invincible heroism which sustained them in the summer of 1944.

There have survived countless graphic accounts of the day-to-day courage in the face of death displayed by the citizens of London, but perhaps one picture is worth a thousand words. This London woman, badly injured by a flying bomb, has been helped to her feet by four solicitous wardens. The expression on her face is the expression on the face of London. Anguished, dazed, unable to grasp the enormity of the madness around her. But still on her feet. The woman does not know where she is. Her eyes are unseeing. All she seems to know is that she is still alive. The threat of the flying bombs was soon removed when the advancing Allied armies found the launching pads and destroyed them. But while they were still operative they struck terror into the stoutest heart.

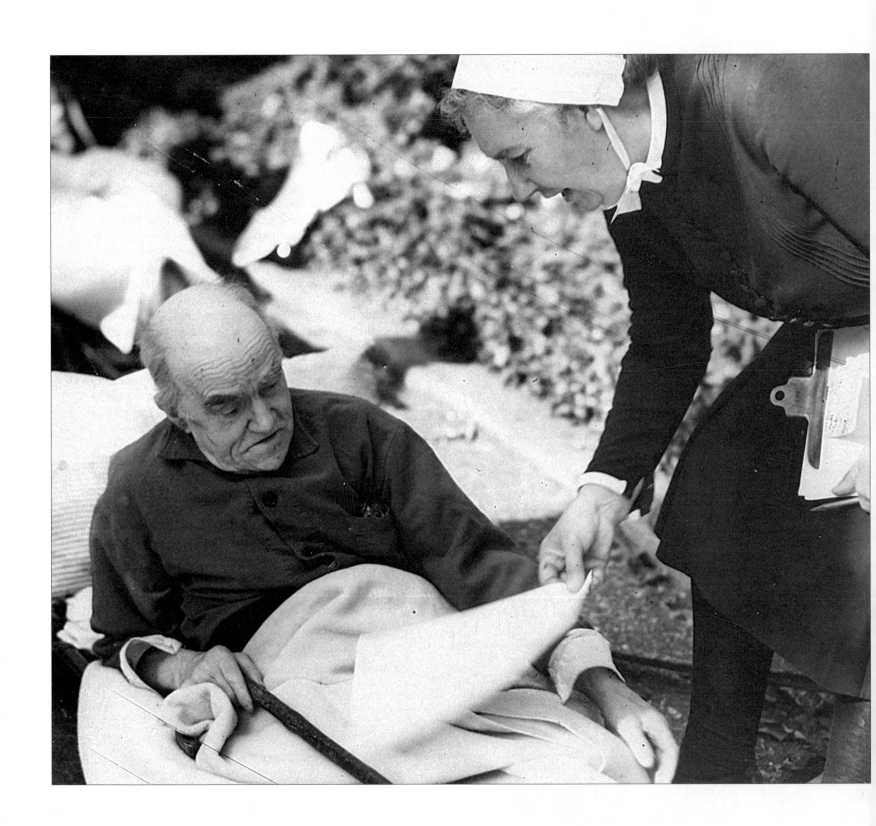

July 26th, 1944. Down in rustic Hertfordshire the Bishop of Everywhere, Mr Bernard Shaw, is celebrating his eighty-eighth birthday with a few spartan vegetarian treats. He predicted this war and predicted its end, and poked such fun at the politicians who led the nation into it that people persist in mistaking him for a comedian. He was one of millions who lived through the period of the flying bomb attacks and survived them unscathed, unlike the old gentleman who must have thought he was secure enough dozing in his hospital bed when the engine cut out, followed by the ominous silence, and then the explosion. The ward he occupied no longer exists, so the matron fusses about his blankets and makes him as comfortable as a venerable gentleman invalid can be in the open air.

Three weeks earlier the carnage had been much worse. Flying bombs came smashing down on three hospitals within the space of twelve hours. In this photograph two patients are being removed by ambulance to one of the local hospitals which has remained undamaged. Their wounds were caused by flying glass, and there is no guarantee that, before the ambulance has reached its destination, it too will not have been blown up, cargo and all, by yet another of the deadly contraptions.

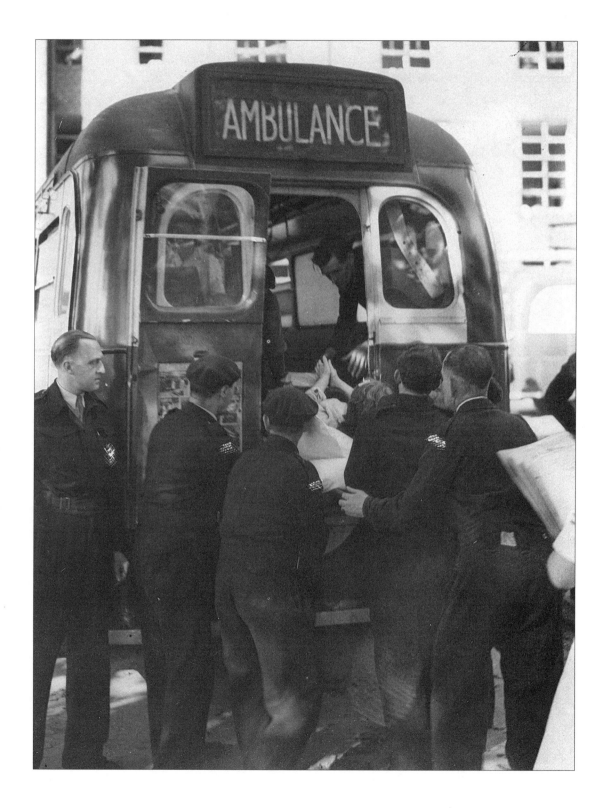

The child's name is Barbara James. Her home, whose wrought-iron decor at the foot of the entrance steps suggests something late Victorian, has been smashed but not destroyed by a flying bomb. A rescue worker has taken her from the house. Where are her parents? The photograph tells us nothing more than that a small child survived. In a sense Barbara James can count herself fortunate. An aerial view of Islington after a flying bomb has crashed down upon it gives a graphic impression of the extent of the damage caused by these eerie raiders. Two blocks of houses have been devastated, trees unrooted, residents blown limb from limb. The population bore its pains stoically, willing on the daily advance of the Allied armies, in the hope that before long the bases of the flying bombs would be captured and destroyed. And indeed they were, and to those who lived through the episode it comes as an anticlimactic surprise to learn that the flying bombs claimed 6,184 lives, nearly all Londoners. By the end of August eighty per cent of the flying bombs which came over were being destroyed. A quarter of the 10,000 that were launched went astray; 7,400 were observed; 1,846 were shot down by fighter planes; 1,878 were destroyed by gunfire. On September 7th the minister responsible announced, 'The Battle of London is over'. Just one day after this fatuous announcement, a new threat became apparent. London became subject to rocket attacks against which there was no defence at all. Plans were made to evacuate the town. The attacks cost the lives of 2,754 Londoners. But then Allied armies overran the launching sites and the danger was past. In the long view, the irresistible ease with which the rockets were able to penetrate all defences tolled the final death knell of Britain as an island. From this point on, the existing concept of an island ceased to exist, at any rate in war.

In the borough of Lewisham, not far from Peckham Rye, stands the London suburb of Forest Hill, on the western bank of the ridge of hills on which the Crystal Palace was built. It is a densely-populated domestic area, and came in for particularly heavy battering in the Blitz and again in the era of the flying bombs. The small houses, some of them detached, were doomed in the event of a direct hit from a flying bomb. Within minutes of the catastrophe, the rescue workers are burrowing in the rubble, hoping to find survivors. And what if they find them? What condition will they be in? What services will be required? One sure bet was that, whether badly injured or merely shaken up, their clothes would probably need a wash. The Women's Voluntary Service improvised a nationwide washing service, which was in effect a mobile laundry. The scene shows a young schoolgirl, unhoused by a flying bomb and without clean clothes, collecting her freshly laundered wardrobe from the intrepid scrubbers and rinsers of the National Emergency Washing Service.

Harry Lillis 'Bing' Crosby, for the previous ten years the world's most popular singer, is seen here at the official opening of London's Stage Door Canteen, a meeting point for serving personnel, who could eat, drink, dance and generally feel the warmth of camaraderie when off duty. The Canteen became a little bit of America stuck in central London, and there was no personality better suited to the inaugural processes than Crosby, who looks slightly unfamiliar without his studio hairpiece. The most prominent feature of the photograph is naturally the gradient of Crosby's ears. It is no impoliteness to make a point of Crosby's ears because he was always making jokes about them himself. In the early days of his stardom the Hollywood makeup mechanics evolved a method of sticking each ear to the side of the head with adhesive tape, but one day, when one ear pinged free in mid-take, Crosby gave the other its freedom and told the studio bosses that from now on they would have to live with his ears just as he did. They agreed. Among the memorable descriptions of himself which Crosby coined when his ears were under discussion, the most popular have been: 'like a taxi with doors open on each side', and 'like a ferret in a high wind'. And although Crosby never made jokes about his toupee, he never seemed bothered about it when appearing before people in real life. He evidently believed that the voice eclipsed all else, and he was right. As the photograph catches him, Crosby is just about to relinquish the lead to another crooner who by D-Day had two recordings in the top five of the British Hit Parade. The songs were *I Couldn't Sleep a Wink Last Night* and *This is a Lovely Way to Spend an Evening*. Readers might like to fill in the name of the singer for themselves. Certainly the young lady modelling the dress and the shoes would have known the answer.

The spherical gentleman with one leg shorter than the other is Morton Downey, a ballad singer of some popularity but rather less aesthetic appeal, whose career in American radio made him a star for two generations. His signature tune was a glutinous ballad called *Wabash Moon*, which he wrote all by himself. When he performed this regrettable piece of sentimentality, Downey not only sang it but whistled it, this ploy being so successful that he later took to whistling in several of his recordings. Like a great many Americans, Downey could wax passionate about Ireland in song, and among his compositions was *That's How I Spell Ireland*. Downey was born in Wallingford, Connecticut. Among his other predictable tendencies was one to sing tear-jerking songs about his mother which would have interested the Freudian school of psychologists had they been aware what was going on, for the oedipal complex was never better expressed than by Downey's successful recordings of *I'll Always Be Mother's Boy* and *Mother's Apron Strings*. Clearly the reason for Downey's mother-love is intimately connected with the way she fed him. In the photograph Downey, who was in London to entertain the troops, is seen asking two London bobbies for directions to the nearest restaurant.

In America by 1944 the oedipal complex was already big business. Mother's Day was second only to Christmas as the cause of tidal waves of lachrymose protestations of fidelity. The serving men in an American Air Force canteen are seen here selecting gifts for mumsie to be posted in time for the great day.

Throughout the war, West Country survivors from the days of Eden Phillpotts and Baring-Gould were subjected to all sorts of disturbing evidence that the old world and its ways were being unceremoniously swept away. But nothing more bizarre could have affrighted their rustic sensibilities than the signs erected by United States garrison commanders faced with the impossible task of holding down their underlings to a reasonable standard of behaviour. The peace of roads which had evolved out of the conventions of a horse-and-cart civilisation were suddenly shattered by the roar of the jeep performing convolutions sometimes not quite within the perimeter of the law. If the contents of the sign are to be respected, an equally common outrage was the sight of soldiers improperly dressed, soldiers parking their vehicles, and soldiers not wearing identity tags. The author of this catalogue of calamity, being too bashful to disclose his own identity, has signed himself mysteriously as 'G-25', which would clearly have made more sense to General Eisenhower than it does to the bewildered soldier in the photograph.

Perhaps the brain behind the system of fines was Major General James Doolittle, commander of the Unites States Eighth Air Force, seen here wearing M. Toulouse-Lautrec's overcoat. Much more sensibly attired for the February weather is King George VI, who regards the massed ranks of military policemen surrounding him and realises there is no escape from the Major General's forces.

After June 6th, 1944, there was a feeling, hard to miss, that the nation was on the march. Desperate battles to win beachheads in Normandy were gradually followed by maps in the newspapers showing the advance of the Allied armies. Beachheads became salients and salients broadened into general advances. Troops were on the move, headed east, and civilian travellers on the trains saw endless evidence of the stream of military men and machines being flung into the battles. No doubt desirous of protecting its valuable fighting men and women from the dangers of railway buffet tea, the authorities usually took the trouble to ensure the presence of the ladies of the Women's Volunteer Service, who are seen here doing their duty by assorted heroes and heroines in a faintly eccentric way. The Bedfordshire branch of the WVS, having exhausted the supply of cups, is reduced to serving tea in jam jars.

Our last glimpse of 1944 is of a consignment of Medical Corps personnel enjoying the last relaxed day they will experience for some time to come. Soon they will be aboard ship headed for the fighting on the continent. Ever since the German invasion of the Soviet Union three years before, the walls and hoardings of the major cities had been scrawled with the demand 'Second Front Now'. At last the request had been granted, but it would be revealing, and no doubt deeply saddening, to know how many of these cheery soldiers will survive the ordeal awaiting them. In the euphoria of the dawning realisation that the war was to be won after all, most civilians hoped that the mopping up would prove a formality. The hope was frustrated and, as 1944 closed, there was much blood yet to be shed.

Bernard Law Montgomery, 1st Viscount Montgomery of Alamein, walks through the streets of London. The ironmongery on his shoulder tabs indicates that on this day he is still a mere lieutenant-general. Even so his aura is powerful enough even now to evoke something close to worship. A charismatic British general who wins battles? No wonder the crowds throng round him, the expressions on their faces telling the story of their hero's exploits in the war. In August 1942, after the Eighth Army had been defeated in the Western Desert by Rommel, Churchill gave him command there. In November 1942 Montgomery, having halted the German advance, defeated Rommel at the Battle of El Alamein, pushing the enemy back all the way to Tunisia, where they surrendered in May 1943. Two months later he was dominant in the successful invasion of Sicily, and was advancing up Italy when he was called to command the invasion of the Allies on the Normandy coast. Under the supreme command of Eisenhower, Montgomery led his forces to victory from the beachheads to Germany itself, receiving the surrender of the German northern armies on May 4, 1945. Later he commanded the British Army of the Rhine, and became Chief of the General Staff. Some idea of the mesmeric effect he had on his countrymen is conveyed by the idolatry of the straw-boatered woman, eager to touch greatness for its talismanic effect.

A group of bronzed Land Army girls performing obscure but vital agricultural duties in the wheat fields of wartime Britain. The Land Army girls were always the most obliging of photographic models, grabbing a hoe or rake or a scythe the moment a camera came into view. After the war many of them remained on the land, but the bulk of the army, fingernails broken, complexions burned to an unfashionable ruddiness, went back to their kitchens and offices, and eventually made some man a good wife.

# 1945

As 1945 opened, the colossal investment of D-Day was paying its dividends. Over a thousand fighting ships, 4,000 assault craft, 1,600 merchant vessels, 13,000 aircraft and more than three-and-a-half million men had been flung into Fortress Europe, and, as the sixth new year of the war dawned, victory seemed within sight. The citizens of southern England, and of London in particular, especially hoped this was so, because the threat of rockets was reviving fears of the worst horrors of the Blitz. In December 1944 the German armies in the west played their last hand by mounting an offensive in the Ardennes and breaking through to a distance of forty-five miles. Command was handed over to Montgomery, who calmly waited until the impetus of the German thrust had faded. By the first week of the new year he was pushing the enemy back. In February Churchill, Roosevelt and Stalin met at the Crimean resort of Yalta where, in less desperate times, Anton Chekhov had gone to live in a vain attempt to find good health. At the Yalta Conference Stalin promised a Russian offensive in the east, at which point fears that the war might still be raging at the end of the year switched to hope of an early victory. For the next three months epoch-making events followed in breathless succession.

The dream of a United Nations Organisation was realised. The American Air Force, by attacking oil supplies, brought the German armies to a standstill. In early March Allied forces crossed to the east bank of the Rhine, and Montgomery penetrated into the Ruhr. By April Alexander's armies were into the Po Valley. On April 12th Roosevelt died. On the 28th Mussolini and his mistress were shot by partisans and their bodies hung from Milan lampposts. The next day German forces surrendered unconditionally to Alexander, and on the day after that Hitler killed himself. On May 4th German armies in the west surrendered unconditionally to Montgomery. Three days later Germany signed an instrument of unconditional surrender. On May 8th Winston Churchill announced the end of the war against Germany. Church bells rang, and floodlight replaced the blackout, even as a wartime song had promised: *I'm Gonna Get Lit Up When the Lights Go On in London.*

But the euphoria of the British was tempered by a sobriety subtly unlike the hysteria at the end of the Great War. The great mass of the people felt that, now that the fighting was done, fighting of a different kind must commence ~ against the appaling privation of the 1930s, against the guilty men of pre-war parliaments, against unemployment and victimisation. Preparations were made for an immediate general election, against Churchill's wishes. What eventually happened to the dream of peace falls outside the frontiers of a book about the war, but among the preparations made by the nation for a return to the ways of peace was a 'demobilization fashion show' for the amazons of the WRNS. The two-piece costume would cost them £12. 10s.

On the outbreak of war, the Queen of England, outraged that Britain should set aside a Day of Humiliation for the success of British arms, informed the Prime Minister that:

*...to say that the great sinfulness of the nation has brought about this war, when it is the selfishness and ambition and want of honesty of one man and his servants which has done it, while our conduct throughout has been actuated by unselfishness and honesty, would be too manifestly repugnant to the feelings of everyone, and would be a mere act of hypocrisy.*

The war in question was not 1939-45, but the Crimean, and the angry monarch not Elizabeth but Queen Victoria. Certain parallels between the two cases are irresistible, but one wonders what Victoria would have made of the idea of the Heiress to the Throne being conscripted into the Armed Forces. In 1945 Princess Elizabeth reached the age of eighteen and became eligible to receive the buff envelope of duty. By April she was training to be an officer in the Auxiliary Territorial Service, and part of her training required the ability to do complicated things with motor cars. 'Somewhere in Southern England' she changes a tyre, and a month later shows her mother, the Queen, some of the secrets of the internal combustion engine.

Victory might seem to be within sight at last, but the rain of death continued to spatter down on to the streets of London. Rockets launched from the continent continued to pose a hideous threat to ordinary citizens, and the advance of the Allied armies became a race against time to locate and destroy the rocket-launching sites before their effect could sway the balance of the outcome. Each rocket cost twenty times as much as a flying bomb and six times as much as a bomber, and there was no practicable defence against it. The danger became so serious that the government considered the abandonment of London and the wholesale evacuation of its population. The situation was saved only because there were too few rockets to cause complete havoc, and they arrived too late in the day. As the armies advanced across France the rockets were destroyed. The last one fell on Orpington in Kent on March 17th – the last of 1,100. The figure of 2,754 deaths sounds minimal in the context of plans for abandoning the capital, but when a rocket did fall, the damage it could cause was indeed frightful.

Only a few days before the rocket phase was ended, one landed in Farringdon Road, reducing half a street to rubble, without, ironically, bringing down what seem to be trolley-bus cables. One lamppost leans its head drunkenly, but the rest of the poles still stand up straight. Most of the debris seems to consist of wood, and it has not taken long for the feet of pedestrians to beat a sort of path through the desolation. For all the danger, people believed by now that the end was in sight, and were willing the invasion forces to speed their advance and end the chapter once and for all. The rocket in Farringdon Street may well have been the last German missile of any kind to do any serious damage to central London.

February, 1945. A rocket arrives and partly destroys a London church. While the ruins are still smouldering, a fireman hauls his hose through the rubble. What froze the London marrow was the lack of any effective defence against the rockets. All sorts of schemes were hastily improvised as the problem of where to house people dispossessed by the rockets posed itself. Some of the homeless took to the air-raid shelters, and on an area of land in Lambeth the special relationship between Britain and the United States took on a bizarre look as American soldiers set to work on the corner of Loughborough Road and Minnet Road. Fourteen hutments of curved asbestos arose, each with two bedrooms measuring ninety square feet, a living-cum-dining room and a kitchen. Each hutment was provided with a gas stove, fireplace and running water. Concrete paths linked the hutments, and, as the photograph shows, the soldiers have even taken the trouble to plant trees, an arboreal touch which justifies the name give to the site: Loughborough Gardens. The soldier-builders undertook to build another twenty-four of these emergency quarters in Lougborough Road, and in the borough more than three hundred.

As the German Army in the West buckled under the strain of the invasion, the sight of prisoners of war became a more familiar one in Britain. Thousands of the captives were put to work in various harmless agricultural pursuits, which seemed like a soft option to many of the survivors of the Blitz, but which was in reality a terrible punishment. To be required to grow things after having been trained to smash things is an interesting form of retribution. Some of the prisoners were placed under the supervision of the United States forces, and in these photographs it is plain that the Americans, too, have reached the conclusion that the most effective form of therapy for a trained destroyer is to require him to build things. Exactly what was being built is not very clear, unless it was a hut to keep the builders seprate from those they had been attempting to exterminate.

The humour of the situation has evidently got home to the vassal in the immediate foreground, who, protected by gloves and boots, is just preparing to take off on a hundred yard sprint race. Possibly the sound of the starter's gun will remind him of his true occupation, but whatever was really going through the minds of these soldiers rendered *hors de combat* by the strategic flair of their masters, captivity was certainly a more enjoyable life than the freedom of dancing with hobnailed boots all over Europe. The laughter on the sprinter's face is the laughter of the man who, having come it much too strong, has been able to take advantage of the comparative gentleness of his conquerors.

And then, quite suddenly it seemed, it was all over. The fighting was done with at last, in Europe anyway. A victory which, in the days of Dunkirk and the Blitz, nobody had really believed in apart from the British themselves, had finally arrived. The mood was euphoric, of course, edging at times, understandably enough, towards hysteria. People went crazy with joy, they cried with pride, they yelled with truculent relief. And yet not quite with the dementia of Mafeking or the bacchanalia of Armistice Day, 1919. There was a difference between this war and all the previous wars in history. For the first time the ordinary citizen had been in the firing line. Celebrants of past victories had been remote from the fighting. Even those residents of the East Coast who, during 1914-18, had glimpsed the occasional zeppelin, had never been under constant bombardment. The great difference this time was that when the residents of mean streets threw up their arms in exultation, it was their own lives they were no longer fearful for. The thought has been too much for the young mother in a London street who holds aloft the crumpled edition of the most precious newspaper she will ever set eyes on.

A U.S. Army sergeant sits on his suitcase in a London street contemplating the most sensational headline of the century. For him the news has a subtly different effect. Apart from reassuring him that the danger is over, it means that in the foreseeable future he will be going home. Once the Japanese have followed the German example, of course.

In Trafalgar Square on the magical May 8th, new manifestations of the 'special relationship' as ladies from the ATS fraternise with gentlemen from the United States Army. The composition of the group, showing a preponderance of the female sex, revives memories in the soldiers' minds of the old vaudeville joke: 'there were three women to every man. Trouble was, they were the same three women!' One of the ladies clutches a soft toy. Another clutches a soldier. Probably it amounts to the same thing.

Very much more information is given in the scenes along Coventry Street. The photographer has been attracted by the crowds, but the real interest lies in the tidal wave of advertising which plasters every façade. At the London Pavilion, Jack Benny and a conspiracy of Hollywood comedians are to be seen in *The Fifth Chair*, an ingeniously unfunny adaptation of a Soviet classic called *The Twelve Chairs*. Audiences are laughing at Benny and com- pany, but this week they would laugh at anything. At the London Hippodrome Ivor Novello is starring in *Perchance to Dream*. If that is too refined, there is George Black's *Happy and Glorious* starring Tommy Trinder. An instalment of Cecil B. De Mille's windbaggery is on offer in the Haymarket, but even more exciting is the offer of Gillette razor blades 'for a better shave'. Drink Gordon's Gin, scream the hoardings. Read the weekly *Illustrated*. Smoke State Express 555. And due east from *The Fifth Chair* may be glimpsed the façade of the Coventry Street Corner House, from whose ramparts the writer of these notes leaned down on the evening of May 8th, 1945, and watched the birthpangs of the Brave New World.

Much was muttered at the time by disgruntled males who might have felt much more gruntled had serving women been allowed to wear even marginally less sensible shoes. The aphrodisiac effect of a lady soldier's clodhoppers or, as in this photograph, of an airwoman's beetlecrushers, was dismaying to say the least. And yet, as the civilian at the far end of the group so eloquently shows, there were worse things than the sensible shoe. This lady, looking vaguely tipsy, has turned up in Whitehall to display shoes with bulbous growths sprouting from each upper, almost as though her despairing attempts to grow tomatoes on them is suddenly bearing fruit. Her hat, too, looking like a winged pizza, compares unfavourably even with the Tyrolean calamity of the heroine in the foreground. As for the rattle she brandishes, and as for the angle to the ground she seems to be trying for, she may well be en route to the pavement in an excess of patriotic tiredness. The only rational figure is that of the RAF officer, although even he has felt obliged to pin a Union Jack on himself as a reminder of which side he is on. A wise precaution in view of the fact that the Tyrolean lady already seems to have aligned herself with a foreign, though admittedly friendly power.

Meanwhile, the reverend gentleman in charge at the Church of St Martin's in the Fields is disturbed in his devotionals by the grinding of jeep gears and the carousing of military personnel just outside the portico. In the Great War, this church played a far grimmer role than it does these days. When shattered young soldiers returned home on leave from Flanders, this was the sanctuary to which they were guided by well-meaning meddlers, since which time the church has been famous for its ever-open door.

The herd instinct guides the huge crowds under Admiralty Arch and along the Mall to Buckingham Palace. Soon after the accession of George VI, the war began, and the new monarch was exposed to doubly increased strain. But he and Queen Elizabeth made themselves the best-loved royal figures of the century, preferring not to be removed from London for their own safety, but choosing to endure the Blitz alongside the population. Later, people would say that this shouldering of wartime duties was the cause of the king's premature death. His Queen has long survived him to become the best-loved lady in the nation. At the far left in the smaller picture stands the ATS officer who will herself be Queen in a few years; at the other end of the line stands her younger sister, just emerging from the childhood appelation of Princess Margaret Rose. And, at the centre, in the large photograph, Churchill, leader of the wartime coalition which has won through to victory even as it has been outstripped in the race for world power by its two giant allies. Soon Churchill will be deposed as the politics of the nation revert once more to inter-party squabbling.

In Trafalgar Square people congregate at the base of Nelson's Column, suitably inscribed for the occasion. Just out of shot the advertising hoardings announce that 'We shall have Moussec wherever we go', and just round the corner to the right of St Martin's in the Fields stands the now-vanished flagship, The Strand Corner House, complete with its giant board proclaiming 'Maison Lyons Chocolates'.

After five-and-a-half years of total war, nobody seemed quite sure exactly when it was all over. The British celebrated its end on May 8th, the Russians on May 9th. Whatever the political machinations behind the confusion, Churchill himself was in no doubt as to the state of things, and on the afternoon of the 8th he was driven at walking pace through exultant crowds to the House of Commons, where he made the formal announcement of victory. Perhaps that sheet of paper held in his hand contains the notes for his speech. When the deed was done, all members of both Houses of Parliament proceeded to St Margaret's, Westminster, to give thanks for victory. Church bells rang out and the floodlights went on, while Churchill looked forward to a quick general election and a reward from a grateful electorate in the form of five years of parliamentary power. The electorate was grateful indeed, but not all that much, and Churchill was deposed in a landslide Labour victory. As he drove to the House on the afternoon of May 8th, none of this could have seemed likely to him.

On the day before Churchill's triumphal descent on the House of Commons, everyone in Britain was poised in expectation of the news. They knew the war was all over in practical terms. Montgomery had received the German surrender on the 4th. On the 7th the instrument of unconditional surrender was signed. But not till the 8th was the official announcement made. At Trafalgar Square on the afternoon of the 7th, four men meet within the paws of one of Landseer's avuncular lions. They are, from left to right, R.T. Westall, R.D. Dowes and G. Yoke of the American forces – all three are from North Carolina – and Harry G. Armstrong, of Perth, Australia. By what currents of war have these four serving men come together? Whatever the answer, ordinary, everyday London hurries by, taking no notice. Are they casual acquaintances, or did they know each other way back when? More likely, have these four heroes made a pact to meet again at the same paw in ten or twenty or thirty years from now? And if so, will they keep their tryst? Almost certainly not. Most of the lifelong friendships forged in the celebrations of May 1945 were doomed to be dissolved in the chaos of demobilisation.

Through a succession of flukes of dynastic circumstance, the British had had a great deal of practise in the elusive art of the street party. In 1935, they had celebrated the Silver Jubilee of King George V and Queen Mary, and took to the streets in an orgy of lemonade and fairy cakes. Within a year the king was dead and the accession of Edward VIII was so eagerly anticipated by millions who mistook him for that nebulous entity, 'a friend of the working man' that once again the street parties were in evidence, even though there was never to be a coronation. Instead, Edward abdicated, and his place was taken by his young brother George, who ascended the throne in the summer of 1937, when, for the third time in three years, the street party received another airing. Usually it required an event empurpled by royalty for the parties to be organised, but a great victory at the end of a bloody war was certainly excuse enough.

All over Britain, in the back streets of great cities, traffic was barred as the trestle tables came out, sheets of white paper were laid along them and fixed by drawing pins. Out from the terraced kitchens came the wooden chairs and the odd bits of crockery, the monumental teapots and the packets of drinking straws. Out came the bowls of quivering, multi-coloured jelly, the hillocks of bread and butter, the almond whirls and other indigestibles, the bottles of lemonade and cream soda and raspberry fizz. And out rolled the barrels of beer, placed at strategic intervals along the street. People might have preferred to celebrate indoors, except that the rooms were not big enough for the purpose. The VE-Day street parties might well have marked the apogee of that institution. The city streets were just the right shape and size for it. The terraced houses meant that everyone knew everyone, the narrowness of the thoroughfares meant that the tables virtually reached from one side of the road to the other. Later, when the cities were smashed by the planners and the developers, the proportions became too giantesque for the street party.

One interesting way of occupying a larger area than the street party usually attempted was to be seen in Kentwell Close in Brockley, a suburb of South London, where the residents of the local blocks of flats arranged the tables to form an emblematic V-sign instead of the ordinary long, thin line. The party is for the children, and the adults have made no provision for themselves.

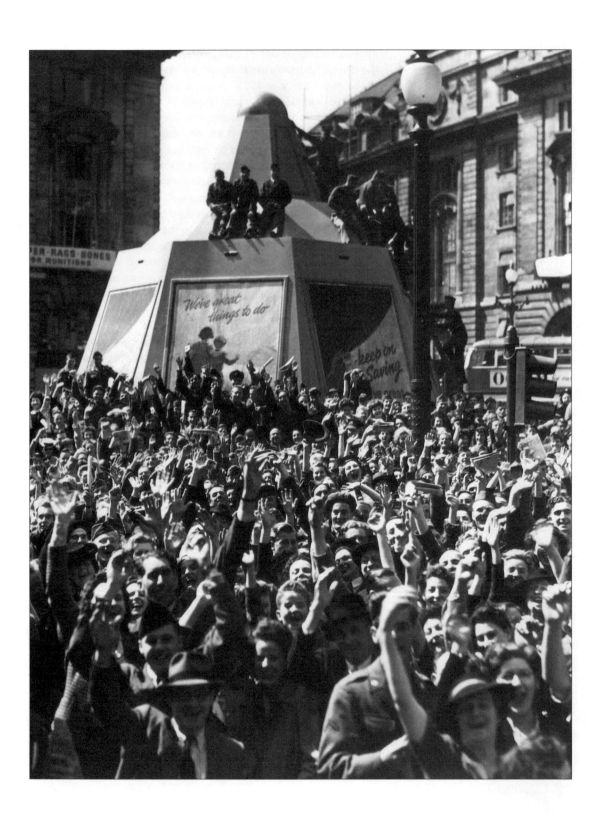

The British had their heroes in the Far East too. Field Marshal Slim was beating back the Japanese Army, and that strange hybrid Wingate, before he was killed, had performed prodigious feats in the jungles. But that theatre of war was mainly America's, simply because the American Empire was located there. It seemed on VE-Day that the Japanese war might become a drawn-out affair, with island-hopping followed by the final invasion of Japan itself. But then came the atomic bomb. Without realising that the known world had vanished forever, that for the first time since recorded history man was able to destroy his own planet, people again turned out to dance in the streets, to embrace strangers, to give thanks for having lived through it all. Nobody could blame them, and who, apart from a few prescient politicians, could have predicted the outbreak of the cold war?

In August 1945, in the wake of the terrifying obliteration of Nagasaki and Hiroshima, American forces in London took to the streets, mingling with the local celebrants and occupying the boarded-up statue of Eros sculpted by a Victorian genius called Alfred Gilbert. The invocations to duty suddenly had no meaning any more. No need to save rags, paper and bones for munitions, no need to keep on saving, and, ominously, no more great things to do. Except perhaps to dance the conga in Piccadilly Circus as a final expression of the special relationship.

Another victory. Another parade. Another drift down the Mall to Buckingham Palace. Last time it had been the German surrender. This time it was the Japanese. Wonder of wonders, every enemy had been beaten from the field. A great, surging sea of citizens washed against the very walls of the Palace, hardly knowing how to express the joy, the relief, the pride, the delirium, of knowing that the land was safe at last. Outside No. 10 Down-ing Street, crowds waited for a glimpse of the Prime Minister, waving, laughing, cheering everyone, including themselves.

But the irony was that the incumbent of No. 10 was no longer Churchill. The Tory Party, keen to capitalise on its leader's prodigious prestige as the war victor, opted for a quick election, with astonishing results. The voters cheered Churchill but voted for Attlee. Amid the wildest euphoria, they could not forget that in 1939 the quality of British life had been nothing to be proud of. Never again the dole, the means test, the unemployment marches, the soup kitchens. This time there would be a government for the people. The Tories were slaughtered to make a Labour picnic. Voting took place on July 5th. Before the end of the month, a few days before the surrender of the Japanese, all the results were in. For the first time in British political history the Labour Party had an overall majority, nearly 400 seats against less than 250 for the combined opposition. The people standing outside No. 10 were announcing one of the momentous victories in British electoral history. A sign of the times was that among the Labour members, representatives of the working classes, forty-six had been educated at Oxford or Cambridge. By mid August the King's Speech to Parliament had announced nationalisation of coal and of the Bank of England. There would be Social Security and a National Health Service. The isles of the Hesperides were looming at long last.

Ever since the American Civil War, the camera had been recording unforgettable images of battle. Had it not been for those images, the nature of modern war would never have come home to those who were left behind. The horror of the trenches in 1914-18 was a perception which owed most to the photographers. The time was to come, in Vietnam, when the movie camera was to fill a nation at war with such revulsion as to bring the fighting to an end. But one of the memorable things about 1939-45 was the thoroughness, and occasionally the inspiration, with which the camera eye caught and preserved for all time some moment in everyday life which happened to express very much more than itself. If the portrait of the aged married couple sitting wearily among the debris of their own lives after an air-raid represents the cruel imbecility of total war, then the portrait of a young lady exhibitionist sailing through the night air in Piccadilly Circus represents the apex of irrational joy and exuberance. The Japs have given in. All day the town has been congratulating itself. Darkness has fallen, and the light from the street lamps is enhanced by a trick of the camera. The chimes of midnight boom out across the river, and still the cheering and dancing goes on. At three o'clock in the morning, someone procures a stout blanket, and somebody else decides to use it as a sort of primitive trampoline. The excuse, if excuse were needed, is that only three hours of world peace have so far passed. As the chimes echoed out, the Japanese War officially ended. Bedlam breaks out at this point. Every motor horn in central London begins to blare. People sound klaxons, blow police whistles, bang drums, crash dustbin lids together. And at the heart of things, alongside the hidden statue of Eros, a young lady volunteers to be flung into the air. The identity of the leaping girl remains unknown. Perhaps the next morning she went to work in the local market, or turned up at the office to type rubbish in triplicate, or put on her uniform and returned to barracks. Perhaps today she is a sedate grandmother with only the dimmest recollection of having been tossed in a blanket on VJ-Night. Somehow it is fitting that we know nothing of her. Like the Unknown Soldier, this unknown leaper enhances her status by her very anonymity. Because she could be anybody, she becomes everybody, expressing the joyousness of a town on the brink of hysteria.

VJ-Day celebrations brought out one of the more romantic items of Fleet Street phrase-making. Trafalgar Square, readers were informed, had become London's most popular dance floor. And so in a way it had. For one thing, admission was free, and for another, there were no insufferable bandleaders to endure. Some of the dances were original, too. A group of stalwarts from the Women's Land Army have invented the new game of tearing a sailor to pieces. The most rigorous investigation has failed to solve the mystery of what the young lady second from the right has gone and got stuck up the back of her pants. In Piccadilly they were dancing different routines again. The glow of a bonfire draws hundreds of carousers, all of them revelling in a recreation which, on an ordinary peacetime day, would get them arrested.

Back in Trafalgar Square the Land Army girls and the dislocated sailor have been swallowed up in the crowds performing the weird and ugly British ritual known as the Hokey-Cokey, whose popularity tonight is enhanced by the fact that there is hardly a Japanese alive who can pronounce it, let alone dance it. But still the most touching effect of all is found in the glimpse of the Land Army girls manhandling the Royal Navy. Behind them, just above a notice advertising a Grand Dance, is an invocation reading 'Keep to the Left'. By voting Churchill out of office the country was doing its best.

London may have hogged the headlines and drawn all the interest of the international news agencies, but deep in the heart of the countryside, too, there was the melodrama of homecoming, its poignancy increased by the fact that in the small villages there were only a handful of native sons of the right age to be conscripted. The village of Oreston is not easy to find on any map. A relief map of South Devon will reveal it to the eagle-eyed, but in this tiny community there took place one of those reunions which sum up the truth of war as it is endured by the families left behind. From the few words of detail accompanying the photograph, and some deductive reasoning arising out of the pictorial evidence, it is possible to reconstruct the past of the uniformed man being feted by his fellow-villagers.

His name is Tucker, and on one of his leaves from the army he married the lady carrying their son and heir, who was born after he had returned to military duties. At some time after that he was captured by the enemy and became a prisoner of war. Today it is May 14th, 1945, and news of his release has reached the village. On the day of his homecoming the children have been equipped with bunting and rehearsed in their duties of providing a ceremonial escort. They have strewn the path of the conquering hero with blossoms, and the two young ladies leading the parade carry dedicatory foliage. The grown-ups stand back and admire the scene, which must be the most exciting the village has ever known. Soon the Labour Government will be formed, the National Health Service will come into being, and Sergeant Tucker's teeth will be given a facelift. For the moment, all is perfect.

And so the Second World War ended in an orgy of tears and laughter, of reunion embraces and the resumption of old ties. The British had an inkling that the pre-war world had gone for good. We were no longer top nation, but in the euphoria of victory that didn't seem quite as important as it would later on. Churchill had told them, 'This was your finest hour'. And so it was; a mountain peak of resource and fortitude which not even the gods themselves could maintain indefinitely. For the moment there were ties to be resumed, fences to mend. The WAAF returning to the bosom of the family is greeted by two nieces who have never seen her before, although the elder of the two puts her finger to her mouth in an effort to work out who this stranger might be.

For the most memorable portrait of the peacemaking, we have to turn to Tulse Hill, on the southeast fringes of London. Gunner Hector Murdock of the Royal Artillery was taken prisoner by the Japs at the fall of Singapore. Of his four-and-a-half years away, three-and-a-half have been spent in a prison camp. He last saw his family when his son John was six months old. Now it is October 14th, 1945. It is his birthday. He cannot return to his home because it was wrecked by a bomb. The family has awaited him in its prefab. He strides down the path towards his wife and son, who leap to embrace him. 'Welcome Home, Hector', reads the banner, and pinned on to the Union Jack is the message: 'Welcome home, dear daddy'. If we are curious as to what the war meant to the British, we have only to study the love and excitement on the face of the small boy as he sprints to grab the father he knows only from the photograph on the sideboard. Soon the bunting will come down, and Hector will put his name on the municipal housing list. But none of the Murdochs will ever forget this moment, which announces more eloquently than any communique – The War is Over.